The Honorable Cause:
A Free South

Twelve Southern Essays

"I am with the South in life or death, in victory or defeat." – Major-General Patrick Cleburne, Confederate States of America

The authors dedicate this book to the Southern People. May they experience true freedom in our lifetimes.

Contents

Introduction 3

There's No Place Like Home, *By James Edwards* 14

Aprons of Resistance: The Role of Southern Women in Modern Dissidence, *By Dixie O'Hara* 33

A Godly Endeavor: Worldview is Everything, *By Harry Bluff*..52

Cousins? Distinctions between Southern Nationalism and White Nationalism, *By Neil Kumar* 79

Become Mythical, Southern Man, *By Father O'Dabney*...110

The Committed Southern Remnant, *By Jude Ruffin*...135

Liberal Democracy vs. Organic Nationalism: A Template for the South, *By Dr. Michael Hill* 152

Reconsidering Our Nation, *By Anne Wilson Smith* ..171

Americanism: Death of the South, *By Rick Dirtwater* 184

Adversaries of the South: The Left's Failed Elites, *By Harmonica*..207

Is the Orthodox Faith the Solution? Building Upon a Southern Ethnos Through True Faith, *By Rebecca Dillingham* 234

Making Secession a Reality: A Strategy, *By Padraig Martin*..264

Introduction

The book you are about to read was conceived in January 2020. At the time, I was a federal prisoner sitting in my cell. I was surrounded by dozens of books sent to me by various supporters, friends, and family. I used my time in prison, well.

Every morning I kept a strict schedule. I would awaken at 0500, make myself a cup of coffee, and read my King James Bible until the sun was up and the yard was made available. I would enter the yard and exercise for approximately two hours. After lunch, I would read a book. I was devouring the equivalent of a 300-page book almost every day. In the evenings, I would find time to speak with some of the older prisoners to learn as much as I could about their various crimes, networks, systems, and schemes (everyone in prison is either "innocent" or the drugs "made" them do it). I hit my rack about 2100 – after count – where I often read until I fell asleep.

The books that I asked my network to send were specific. I wanted to strengthen my knowledge of revolutions, rebellions, and insurgencies. I wanted to learn what succeeded and why some failed. Of particular interest to me were books on Irish Nationalist history (my genetic lineage). I studied men like Michael Collins, Tom Barry, Ernie O'Malley, Arthur Griffith, Eamon de Valera, and Daniel Breen. In addition, I asked for books on the Iranian revolution (the focus of my graduate thesis in 2006), Hezbollah, Hamas, and other anti-Western, Islamic resistance movements. Finally, my other topic was Marxist inspired revolutions. I studied the Bolsheviks, Maoists, and the myriad of movements that seemed to intermix communism and nationalism.

The purpose of my studies was targeted. I would emerge from prison a more knowledgeable and better prepared advocate for my people. I entered prison as a Southern Nationalist. I would use the time the government gifted me to strengthen my knowledge, skillsets, and value for the movement. I knew that my prosecution was related to my participation at Charlottesville. In fact, so pathetic were the charges against me (i.e., making false statements to the US Government in connection to a military sub-contract I held in 2014/15), that I was fined $400 by a federal judge and sentenced to six months in prison, four more months of house arrest, and three years of probation (the maximum allowable by the sentencing guidelines based on the federal government's awkward points system). In other words, the very little they had on me amounted to a cumulative minor slap. This was retribution for committing the crime of "wrong think." I determined to make prison yet another graduate school – one from which I would leave more dedicated to my cause than ever before.

I practiced Russian and Spanish, thanks to my conversations with inmates. I finished the Bible, reading it cover-to-cover. I proselytized Southern Nationalism to the inmates with whom I found occasion to have in-depth conversations. In other words, I built myself into a more complete Nationalist and anti-government activist.

Using the time provided, I came to several conclusions as to the best way to contribute to the Southern Nationalist cause. First, it was clear that we needed to define ourselves in a better way. The movement was handcuffed by the mistakes of the past and the ability of our adversaries to characterize us. Second, we needed to work on funding for the cause. Too many men had their lives ruined by leftist agitators through doxing; my own life included. We had to have anti-fragile means of producing an income. Thirdly, we needed to change our strategy from one that involved direct action to one that was more subtle and nuanced.

The latter was critical. We – Nationalists of various stripes – keep fighting an enemy on their own terms and keep losing. By losing, I do not mean physically. Thrashing the antifa is easy to do. They wilt quickly upon first strike. Rather, I mean that they control all the mechanisms of power, and consequently can direct law enforcement, judges, and other elements of the establishment's Praetorian Guard to come after us at will. We needed a new way to achieve a singular objective of dismantling these United States and realizing balkanization. If we want to end the United States as we know it today, we cannot do it by punching pseudo-Marxists in the face and spending time in prison. We need a smarter way.

I committed myself to these objectives in prison and I have kept to those commitments since I got out. This book is a realization of one of those goals – "defining ourselves in a better way." It seeks to take back the narrative. We have a United States on the precipice of collapse, all she needs is a simple push. We need to provide the appropriate ideological outlook for those who seek an alternative to the status quo. Southern Nationalism is the alternative they seek.

The beauty of the current environment is that the United States government is making every classic mistake of a country about to implode. The study of any successful revolution clearly points this out. The expansion of the police state, the exploitation of media mechanisms to suppress unflattering or contradictory information, the overreaction to dissent, and the targeting of the popular genetic majority through weaponizing minority grievances has always led to a country's collapse. The only thing we lack as a true revolutionary movement is a complete collapse in democratic trust. As long as Americans trusted that their vote mattered, we had an uphill battle. It is hard to get even an enraged citizenry to embrace change when they believe they can vote their way out of an unacceptable political situation. Thankfully, the US government decimated that trust.

Exploiting the election outcome of 2020 – whether you believe the election was stolen or simply have concerns – is an incredible tool. More than half of the United States believes bad actors ended the only peaceful outlet of resistance for a disaffected people. Complementing this belief in overt election theft is the idea that leftist elites are manipulating illegal immigration to effect systemic change through mass voter fraud. By denying common sense ID laws, leftists – whether intentional or not – are feeding the flames of distrust as it pertains to the system. Every other democracy in the world has some mechanism of showing "proof" as it pertains to the right to vote. Yet American leftists continue to oppose this simple measure that inspires trust in the system. The only logical conclusion is that such a denial is a willful desire to impact election outcomes by nefarious means. This all translates to a fantastic opportunity for the spread of Nationalism. They are giving us the fuel AND the matches.

Nearly half of the United States voted for Donald Trump, and the United States ruling class called them "enemies" on MSNBC, CNN, and Fox News. Even better for us, when those voters protested the results on January 6, 2021, the extreme overreaction of what was largely a peaceful, albeit raucous protest, was a propaganda windfall. Civic Nationalists – those who believe law (e.g., the Constitution) not race defines a national identity – suddenly found themselves targeted by the same police state they supported over the preceding years, back when that same police state attacked "racists." More astoundingly, as arrests and prosecutions mounted for pro-Trump protesters, members of the radical Left were released from jails and their 2020 riot-related charges were dropped. The US government gave us an even greater gift than we could have ever hoped.

Historically, there has never been a country that survived the impulsive suppression actions of a reactive government. From Bourbon France to Colonial America… from the Shah's Iran to the Soviet Union… from Hashemite Iraq to Peronist Argentina – they are all gone. The United States as we know it today is operating on borrowed time and they gave us all the rhetorical ammunition we need to facilitate its dismantlement.

Due to these extraordinary circumstances and the wonderful mistakes of our ruling elites, Southern Nationalists enjoy an opportunity they have never really had. Support for secession is growing throughout the United States. We need to articulate a message and vision that resonates in the hearts of Southerners. We need to inspire them to walk away. That is the purpose of this book.

For those being introduced to the concept of Southern Nationalism, it is simply a belief that the Southern people are a unique ethnic group on the North American continent, derived from a rich European heritage – namely Anglo and Celtic – with a unique Christian moral foundation. Southerners have their own traditions, history, and culture. They have a right to preserve that rich heritage and ethnic identity. Most Southern Nationalists believe that the only way to preserve that heritage is to secede and rule ourselves.

This book seeks to provide the readers a deeper understanding of that ethnic identity and how Southern independence might take shape. Twelve authors collaborated in the making of this book, including myself. These authors were chosen because of their known commitment to the Southern cause. Some are using pseudonyms. Some are not. I approached each of the authors to contribute to a collection of essays that we – the collection of contributors – hope will provide a better understating of Southern Nationalism, in the words of Southern Nationalists.

The title, "The Honorable Cause: A Free South," was designed with input from all of the contributors to this project. It directly assails the idea that there was ever a "Lost Cause." None of us believe that the cause is lost. Rather, we believe it needs to be reinvigorated because the idea of Southern independence is honorable. The Irish tried sixteen previous attempts at securing their freedom from the British before they achieved independence on the seventeenth try. To date, the South has only tried once. It is time to try again – preferably by peaceful, political means. This book covers not only why Southern independence can be achieved, but how that might happen.

What you will not find are long, racist or antisemitic screeds. That is not the purpose of this book. We are not here to denigrate someone else. We are here to elevate our people and show them that they would do better divorced from the American Empire. You may or may not agree with the viewpoints or solutions of the authors. You may find yourself informed, shocked, amused, or angered. The more emotional the reaction, the better. We want to stimulate your mind, but we really want to inspire your heart.

Thank you for reading our words. Thank you for taking the time to explore our thoughts. As 2024 approaches, we know that 2023 must be a year of action. This is the first in a series of initiatives aimed at reclaiming the narrative and winning for our people. They need us more than ever. We are here for them.

Deo Vindice!

Padraig Martin

There's No Place Like Home, *By James Edwards*

"The South is a land that has known sorrows; it is a land that has broken the ashen crush and moistened it with tears; a land scarred and riven by the plowshare of war and billowed with the graves of her dead; but a land of legend, a land of song, a land of hallowed and heroic memories. To that land every drop of my blood, every fiber of my being, every pulsation of my heart, is consecrated forever. I was born of her womb; I was nurtured at her breast; and when my last hour shall come, I pray God that I may be pillowed upon her bosom and rocked to sleep within her tender and encircling arms." – U.S. Senator and Tennessean Edward Ward Carmack

It was a beautiful spring morning in 2007 when I walked out the front door to find a limousine waiting in my driveway. It had been sent by CNN. The network had arranged first-class car and air transportation to New York City, as well as posh hotel accommodations in Central Park, for what would be the first of a series of appearances that I would make for them as a television commentator. On that night, I was being brought on to participate in an hour-long panel debate about self-segregation.

Primetime. Live. 8:00 p.m. EST. Their most popular show at the time. Back in those days, I was still introduced simply enough as a conservative talk radio host.

After it was over my driver asked where I wanted to go, so I asked him to take me to Times Square. I do like to travel, and I enjoy fine things. But I still vividly recall more than 15 years later walking to a restaurant in Manhattan and thinking about the red dirt hills of Pontotoc County, Mississippi. I don't know why the birthplace of my maternal grandparents came to mind in that moment, but the thought was warm and comforting. I'd have much rather been there.

That might sound strange to some people who can't understand our unwillingness to abandon our customs, folkways, and symbols. But this is who I am and it's personal. I cannot be separated from it, and I want my three children to cherish our Southern heritage and love the land from whence we came as much as I do. In fact, I make a point to take annual day trips with my family to visit the rural Southern towns that gave birth to their great-grandparents. The first thing we do upon any given arrival is visit Confederate Square to see the beautiful monument that is proudly featured at its center.

There are hundreds of such monuments that serve as the heart of town and county squares across Dixie, but in Pontotoc, the inscription reads, "Love's tribute to the soldiers who marched beneath the stars and the bars and were faithful to their duty, this monument is erected in grateful remembrance." The front simply reads, "Our Heroes: 1861-1865." The sentry atop the monument stands faithfully on his eternal watch.

I never feel more at peace than when I am there. Life moves at a slower pace. There is an almost otherworldly calm that comes from talking with the rural townspeople and eating dinner at one of the family-owned diners before visiting the town museum, which is free of charge and located inside the small post office.

After spending time in town, we make the ten-minute drive over to the community of Thaxton, which is essentially comprised of just a handful of buildings: a town hall, a small grocery store with a single gas pump, and a couple of churches. I am extraordinarily proud of my family's history and way of life. I am always taken back to my childhood when I revisit the tiny community center at which so many of our reunions used to be held, before so many of my kin went on to receive their heavenly reward. The place still looks as it did in some of my earliest memories. The 1950 senior class photo of my grandmother remains hanging on the wall. There is a basketball court with wooden backboards that hover over the same floor that my grandfather played on so many decades prior. There is something bittersweet and endearing to visit a place where time stands still. It puts my spirit at ease.

My grandparents, who were born in Thaxton before moving to Memphis to find work, were the children of poor sharecroppers. They themselves also picked cotton before and after school. During the winters, my grandfather huddled with his brothers and sisters while they slept to stave off the cold. He told me stories of being able to see the stars through the roof of their ramshackle house. The world would have me believe that this is White privilege.

There is no virtue in poverty, but there *is* in sacrifice and hard work. This generation engaged in harder work than I have ever known, which is just one of the reasons I take great pride in being able to visit the land that they farmed before paying respects at the graves of my great-grandparents. Even though my children can never know them, it means so much to be able to teach them about who they were and raise them in the same traditions and ethics that were handed down to me through the generations. These were great people who left a legacy, and it is vitally important to me that my children be raised to love one another and their ancestors. A deep reverence for our people is fundamental, and my wife and I have instilled it in each of them since birth. Sons and daughters of the South are never too young to learn about heroes, especially the ones in our own family tree who fought for the Confederacy. To be directly descended from this line of brave and fighting Christian men is a patrimony that is worthy of preservation.

Yes, the South *was* right, but so too have been others throughout history. It's not simply the right and the wrong that compels me to stand for my people. It's the birthright of having blood in my veins that flowed from the last group of men who fought that way on this continent. Now *that's* something special. I thank God for Him having seen fit to allow me to come into this world as a Southern man, and to have been born and raised in Dixie. What is love if not sacrificing for your family and standing at the ready to defend their honor?

I routinely hear friends and acquaintances mention the high-ranking Confederate officers in their lineage. So much so that I often joke about being descended from the only private in the

Confederate army. On my paternal side, my great-great-great grandfather was a private in Mississippi's 4th Cavalry Battalion. As a young boy, my parents would regularly take me to visit that set of great grandparents in Corinth, Mississippi. I was even lucky enough to have seen the blood-stained saddle that belonged to my heroic ancestor so many years prior.

It was from Corinth that he marched to Shiloh. During that legendary battle, he shared the field with one of Dr. Michael Hill's ancestors. I got my start in politics by working on Pat Buchanan's presidential campaign in 2000. Years later, Buchanan shared with me a story about one of his own great-great grandfathers. Cyrus Briscoe Baldwin was a first lieutenant in the 31st Mississippi Infantry. He lived in Okolona, Mississippi, and died in service on June 26, 1862. Okolona is situated practically within walking distance of both Thaxton and Corinth. Dr. Hill once remarked to me during a radio interview that his ancestral memory was stirred the moment he first visited Scotland. I sometimes wonder whether those of us who are committed to keeping the flame aren't predestined to find each other during our lifetimes.

I was born 115 years after General Lee's surrender at Appomattox, and I tell you that my eyes swell with emotion whenever I hear "Dixie" being played, or when I read accounts of the gallant attempt those men made in their war to protect their loved ones from federal oppression and tyranny. It is a feeling that only a Southerner can know, and it transcends time and space.

Speaking of family, some years ago one of my listeners mailed to me a copy of a letter sent by the Comptroller of the State of Florida to his great grandmother, who was by that time (December 20, 1933) a widow. Her husband had been a Confederate veteran and the letter accompanied his pension check.

State of Florida
Comptroller's Office
Tallahassee, FL

December 20th, 1933

Mrs. Sarah [last name redacted]

Tampa, Florida

Dear Friend:

I consider it quite fortunate on my part in being selected as the official charged with the responsibility of mailing you the enclosed pension check. It is a rare privilege and a pleasure to forward you this token of appreciation of the great State of Florida.

I sincerely wish you and yours a very Merry Christmas and a surprisingly Happy New Year.

Personally, I feel the debt of gratitude owing you by the commonwealth of this state cannot be estimated in material wealth and therefore, cannot be composed by mere payment of money. It is a liability that cannot be expressed in dollars; but it can be enshrined in the sacred archives of tradition; and by teaching the succeeding generations that by your actions, experience, and devotion to a sacred principle you have proved that God does not force us into deep water to drown us, but to cleanse us. And that adversity is the trial of principle without which one hardly knows whether or not he is honest; unless, like

How could the world so ardently hate people capable of composing such awe-inspiring sentiments? Ultimately, because they hate Jesus Christ, and Jesus told us that since they hate Him, they will also hate us (John 15:18-25). But most immediately, because the faith of our fathers makes us effective opponents of those who desire to enslave people to debt and to governance which does not produce societies fostering industry, accomplishment, justice, safety, and courage — all of which are hallmarks of traditional Southern culture. If they can purge faith and family from our hearts, then it's only a matter of time before they can dominate and destroy us; and with their toughest opposition out of the way, they can dominate the world.

However, when one is tethered to eternal truths you will feel the same willingness to sacrifice yourself for your people that Paul did: "For I could wish that myself were accursed from Christ for *my brethren, my kinsmen according to the flesh*" (Romans 9:3); you'll feel the same imperative to protect your genetic line, as Abraham did when he told his servant, "But thou shalt go unto *my country, and to my kindred, and take a wife unto my son Isaac*" (Genesis 24:4); and you'll fear the displeasure of God, Who said through Paul, "But if any provide not *for his own, and specially for those of his own house,* he hath denied the faith, and is worse than an infidel." (1 Timothy 5:8)

Now middle-aged, when looking back on my life up to this point, I grow more thankful each day that I was born into a family with a father and mother who raised me in church. I spent every weekend during the early years of my life either marinating on a pew or visiting relatives in the Magnolia State. The lessons learned in both places on those formative Sundays made me a better man and a more effective advocate. Our lifelong pastor also played an important role in my development, and we are still dear friends to this day. It all still holds a special place in my heart, and I shudder to think what paths I might have taken had it not been for the solid foundation upon which my upbringing was built. I was very fortunate to have had the stability of a nuclear family, parents and grandparents who always let me know how much I was loved, the importance of our cultural and spiritual heritage, and the difference between right and wrong. In this nest, I flourished. These are the communities and the homes that we seek to restore.

By the time I reached adulthood, I knew that serving as an advocate for our people group, what I consider to be our extended family, bridges the gap between our distant ancestors and our future progeny. We fight for our past, present, and future and such a connection gives our finite time on this earth fulfillment. How utterly meaningless the life of a vapid American consumer must be.

Even struggle can be animating and fulfilling. The attacks and defamations that we suffer should be welcomed because it builds character. As that letter I shared with you stated, without adversity you don't know whether or not you're honest. As a friend of mine recently opined, great men are never made except through great trials. Adversities aren't obstacles, but rather our greatest opportunities – to get better, forge our character, work harder, become smarter, and prove our worth.

You won't know what you're made of until your time comes and you face a decision. Our Southern forebears knew it all too well. When you face a crucible with steadfast resolve you have honored your ancestors and solidified your standing as a man. The immortal words of Gen. Patrick Cleburne have oftentimes steeled my own resolve. As he put it, "If this that is so dear to my heart is doomed to fail, then I pray heaven may let me fall with it, while my face is toward the enemy and my arm is battling for that which I know to be right."

I'm not going to tell you that those who hate us are incapable of harming you. They can, and they do. They will libel you, slander you, and even cause you economic distress. But there is one thing that they cannot take from you and that is your dignity and self-respect - unless you put it on offer. As Davy Crockett once remarked, "Be always sure you are right - then go ahead." We must never apologize or capitulate about things we know to be true to those who seek our destruction and ruin. We dishonor ourselves and bring shame to our name by shrinking from our duties during times of hardship. It should also be remembered that the sacrifices we must make pale in comparison to the sacrifice of blood and bone that were given by our betters.

One Southern woman, whose name is only remembered by God, gave such a sacrifice. On June 3, 1864, Robert Audry of Company B, 111th Illinois Infantry, mailed a letter to his father, describing some recent action his unit had seen.

> *Dear Father,*
>
> *I take pen in hand to let you know that I am well. We are encamped near Dallas, Georgia where we found the enemy in force on the 26th. The 111th was in the front line of the breastworks, and we drew a hot fire from the rebs until about 4 o'clock when the enemy viciously charged our works. We poured hot fire into their ranks and several times their lines broke, but they rallied again and came on with guns blazing and flags waving. They fought like demons and we cut them down like dogs. Many dead and dying Secesh fell prisoner.*
>
> *I saw 3 or 4 dead rebel women in the heap of bodies. All had been shot down during the final rebel charge upon our works. One Secesh woman charged to within*

several rods of our works waving the traitor flag and screaming vulgarities at us. She was shot three times but still she came. She was finally killed by two shots fired almost simultaneously by our boys. Another She-Devil shot her way to our breastworks with two large revolvers dealing death to all in her path. She was shot several times with no apparent effect. When she ran out of ammunition, she pulled out the largest pig-sticker I ever seen. It must have been 18 inches in the blade. When the Corporal tried to shoot her she kicked him in the face, smashing it quite severely. Then she stabbed three boys and was about to decapitate a fourth when the Lieutenant killed her. Without doubt this gal inflicted more damage to our line than any other reb. If Bobby Lee were to field a brigade of such fighters, I think that the Union prospects would be very gloomy indeed for it would be hard to equal their ferocity and pluck.

Our regimental losses were about 6 killed and 10 wounded including Lt. Col. Black who was slightly wounded I believe in the thigh. Please give my best regards to all inquiring friends and love to the family.

Your Devoted Son,

Robert Audry, 111th Ill. Regt. Vols.

Perhaps it was such a tale that led W.E.B. Du Bois to famously write that, "Across this path stands the South with a flaming sword."

One thing I do know is that a man who refuses to defend his family's name is no man at all. How dare the vandals of multiculturalism assume that they can cast aspersions on our people and our folkways. Of course, having a separate culture from that of your surrounding geographical areas is the very prerequisite for being a separate nation. Still to this day the South does possess that, especially the rural South.

We still have unique traditions, faith, heroes, history, and even our own suffering, which is especially important because a group of people that suffers together is bound together. Each component is essential to the uniqueness of the Southern nation. It's personal and if you allow yourself to become separated from all of that, all the things that make you who you are, then you're already dead. You may be breathing. You may be going to and from work and performing various tasks. But that's not the same as being truly alive.

Thankfully, those who read this book are not yet dead in either body or soul. *Dum spiro spero* from Latin reads, "While I breathe, I hope." I hope that our people will rise up and reclaim their destiny. I believe that we still can. Dixie and everything about her must endure for our posterity. It's our home, after all, and there is no place like it.

About the Author: James Edwards serves as the creator and host of The Political Cesspool, a syndicated AM talk radio program. When not interviewing newsmakers, Edwards is no stranger to making news himself, having appeared as a commentator many times on national television. Over the course of the past two decades, his groundbreaking work has also been the subject of articles in hundreds of publications around the world.

Edwards' book, <u>Racism, Schmacism: How Liberals Use the "R" Word</u>, was published in 2010. In 2016, Mr. Edwards was listed by a well-funded leftist "media watchdog group" alongside Ann Coulter as one of the "Top 20 right-wing media fixtures" responsible for Donald Trump. Hillary Clinton later named him as an "extremist" who would shape our country.

Aprons of Resistance: The Role of Southern Women in Modern Dissidence, *By Dixie O'Hara*

My grandma's kitchen in Southern Alabama smelled like heaven. As a little girl, I was always excited to don my own apron and join her in the kitchen. It was nearly identical to the one she wore. There was something magical about standing in the center of the scents and excitement. I would spend all day cooking next to her. I learned the flavors of my people licking stir spoons and mixing bowls. It is in the kitchen where I learned how to make biscuits, how to feed a family, and the important role of women in the South.

The beauty of the South is often born from the tragic pain her people have suffered. In this regard, Southern women and Southern food share so much in common. Our female ancestors watched their menfolk head to a conflict from which many would not return. Left to fend for themselves throughout the War Between the States, Southern women had to survive the cruelty of war relying upon one another. As a Northern army swept through their homelands, Southern women watched their homes burned, their children starve, their livestock stolen, and many suffered the indignities of satisfying lustful Yankee soldiers against their will. Southern women relied upon one another throughout this traumatic period.

The decade after the War was another era of deprivation and occupation. The heartless vengeance exacted upon Southerners during Reconstruction remains unrivaled in the history of modern warfare. Entire families would vanish from a wasteland made at the hands of Northern oppressors. Revisionist historians like to laud Yankee largess in the post-War years. Entire graveyards in the South betray that lie. Again, Southern women held together the family unit and became the cultural glue of the South at a time of humiliation.

Whereas the South is an American region that played a crucial role in the formation of these United States, 1860 – 1877 was a defining moment in the ethnic composition of Dixie. Mothers from this timeframe would ensure their young sons and daughters never forgot that which they endured nor the names of the perpetrators. This knowledge was passed down generationally until the federal government took charge of all education beginning in 1980. Southern food, however, remains the cultural reminder of a people who were assaulted, occupied, and remain oppressed by a heartless foreign government.

It is in the poverty of the ingredients, the wealth of our soil, the unforgiving weather, and the love of our people that our cuisine is distinct from the rest of those other Americans. It is also our ethnic composition that creates a rich tapestry of flavors – from the Anglo coast to the Celtic Appalachian interior to the Mediterranean Gulf (French in Louisiana; Spanish in Florida, Alabama, and Texas). Our history is carved into simple dishes, providing a framework within which the combination of recipes shares both similarities and flavorful differences under the same named dish.

Black-eyed peas remind us of Sherman's "March to the Sea." Grits keep a working man and a growing boy full. The abundance of pork finds its way into many dishes, whether by virtue of country ham, hog jowls, or true Carolina barbeque. Cajun food informs the palate of Louisiana's vibrant historical confluences. Royal Red shrimp remind Southerners of their unique coastal heritage. But it is the humble biscuit that is my favorite. It was my introduction into a legacy of Southern femininity and the responsibility I have inherited to my family.

Biscuits in the South can be a complement to a meal, or they can be a main course. They are simple and easy to make, yet they require some love to make them right. I prefer making my biscuits in a cast iron pan. Both cast iron and biscuits can be found in every Southern kitchen – along with lots of butter and bacon fat.

The biscuit is a poor man's meal. The primary ingredients of which are flour, milk, and butter. Throughout the South, with the exception of Florida, one can find winter wheat flour. Southern winter wheat is different than the all-purpose flours found in other regions within these United States, one of the many reasons Yankee chefs often fall flat when attempting Southern cuisine in their colder climates. It may also have to do with their lack of heart.

There is a joy that comes from memories of me as a little girl making biscuits with my grandma. It is indescribable to watch your granddaddy, father, and uncles smile as they eat them. A girl's heart can burst when she is told her biscuits are just like grandma's. That is tradition captured in a moment of emotional memory.

Southern women have kept their families fed throughout times of extraordinary hardship. Flour is cheap. So too are many of the ingredients you will find in the South. But the heart is rich, and the traditions are too important. The family is the root of Southern culture and a woman's kitchen is a critical epicenter. Only her heart is more important within the home.

Soul Food is often equated to Southern food. The two are different, but Yankees rarely understand those distinctions. I respect the black mothers and grandmothers who pass down their traditions toward the girls in their families. Our foods and flavors are born from hardships that we find within our own lineages. Each recipe denotes a time in history under which our respective but distinct peoples have suffered. These are related foods – cousins, as such – born in the agrarian simplicity of Dixie.

Cuisine, however, is uniquely nationalistic. In fact, it may be the most acceptable form of nationalism on the planet. Italian food, Greek food, French food, Japanese food, Thai food… all of these varieties of flavors may or may not share ingredients or occasional similarities, but each is very different. The nationalist profile is expressed on a plate. Children eventually crave foods mothers introduce to do them at an early age. When they are adults, they either come home for those same flavors, they cook those flavors themselves, or they find someone who can do so. Whereas American food can be found nearly everywhere, they are generally bastardizations of European recipes or dishes. Southern food is influenced by our European heritage, but it stands on its own. It is an expression of Southern Nationalism.

The South's soil plays a big role in defining ingredients used to create the dishes we serve, and each state is different. Northern Florida's sandy soil provides a very different availability of vegetables and herbs than its northern neighbor, red clay Georgia. North Carolina's Piedmont is distinct from North Carolina's coast. Even the composition of grits changes from Southern country to Southern country. Yellow "corn" grits, coarse white grits, stone ground grits, and hominy absorb flavors and provide textures that change regionally throughout the South. In essence, our food becomes the personification of the soil.

This circles back to the importance of food to the Southerner and her family. It is more than sustenance for its own sake. Food becomes the centerpiece of church fellowships. The community meets one another after a Baptist sermon or a Methodist service with dishes that are meant to be recognized and complimented. This is not a matter of brining a few pans of fried chicken to a meeting of hungry parishioners. This is a matter of bringing something for which the others enjoying that food will remember or share quiet thoughts about the quality.

"Mary Lou's chicken was good, but it was missing something… Sue Ann's cornbread was so dry, the trees were bribing the dogs… Maize tries, bless her heart…" A church fellowship can get far more ruthless than the cooking shows I enjoy on the Food Network.

Dishes can also exemplify distinctions of family status, or they can remind the family of humbler times. As the South grows wealthier, it is easy for Southerners to forget their more impoverished roots. Most of us are within a generation or two in which our homes were far smaller, simpler, and less ostentatious. Our cuisine reminds us that we did not always enjoy the luxuries of minor mansions in the suburbs of Atlanta or Nashville.

It is hard for some to remember a time when spices were a rarity in a less populated, less affluent South. Recipes remind us. You will not find harissa, curry, or black truffle salt among mawmaw's recipe cards. I have these spices in my kitchen and I explore with infusions of Southern recipes and exotic flavors today, but somewhere in my heart, I know my grandma is giving me a side-eye from Heaven.

The importance of those recipes and traditions come with a feminine responsibility to our people. For all ethnicities around the world, women are the most critical cultural arbiters. This is not to diminish the importance of men. But women, by virtue of their early childrearing responsibilities, play an outsized role in the continuation and perseverance of traditions, morals, and identity.

Throughout history, women raised children from the point of infancy with minimal male involvement. This begins with breastfeeding – literally the first and most important food a woman can provide her child. In fact, in the womb, the introduction of foods, spices, and preferences begins forming by virtue of the mother's choices. But a woman's breast is the child's first external introduction of the importance of his mother to himself. It is also the most important connection of the female responsibility to feed her family, beginning with that newborn feeding.

The beauty of breastfeeding is that it is a bond through food. It is an entirely feminine act. There are many great male chefs who can produce exquisite Southern meals, but they will never provide life sustaining sustenance to an infant. That is a woman's exclusive prerogative by virtue of her God given and biologically unique gift.

From the moment a mother gives birth to her child, she is drawn to support her child's most profound need. There is something intrinsically natural about the act itself. Whereas some mothers and babies struggle initially, without virtue of advanced practice or training, breastfeeding simply happens. Eventually the child finds his or her mother and the mother produces milk. It is from this very moment that children begin to learn human basics. Expounded upon more broadly, the closeness of the mother to the child will translate to a variety of other traits and traditions – from temperament to lullabies.

Standing at my skirt, my children learned to experience life through my eyes and flavors from my kitchen. They learned how to speak through my soothing words at night or my interaction through the day. They learned to speak like Southerners by hearing me speak. This was reinforced by friends and family, but the first "y'all" they ever heard was my own.

Life lessons are taught by watching mama. My children learned how to distinguish happy, angry, and sad tones through my voice. They heard me pray. They watched me interact with their father. They watched me in the kitchen. Whereas fathers are very important to this growth, children have an immediate bond with their mothers that is hard to put into words. It is just an experience.

Food is a manifestation of that experience. Various flavors over time have been introduced to the family. Some of those flavors were a little too advanced for the simpler, immature palates of little children. But for the most part, over time, they learned to explore a range of tastes that all came back to the South in some way.

The nationalistic expression of food combines blood – family – and soil – the very food itself – to create a unique identity. This is definitionally ethnic. Italian women use semolina flour made from Italian durum wheat to create pasta dishes from recipes passed down generationally to feed their families. Southern women use flour made from Southern grown soft red winter wheat to make biscuits from recipes passed down generationally to feed their families. These are ethnic distinctions that transcend all attempts to supersede and homogenize peoples into an undistinguished mass of uniformity.

Recent attempts to destroy Southern iconography and unique identity have focused on attacks upon our monuments. They believe ripping out the names of brave men from town centers will somehow kill Dixie's stubborn determination to remain exceptional within the American context. They do not understand the South. Like our Celtic forebearers who once kept their traditions secret around firesides in the mountains of Scotland, the only way to destroy the South's identity is to rip apart and destroy the South's strong family connections. Statues do not define us. Our culture defines us.

While it is true, regional accents are being washed away by bland Midwestern dialects thanks to mass media, we still hold onto idioms and vernacular. "Cattywampus," "y'all," and "that dog won't hunt," does not have the same ring from a Michigander or a Bostonian. These terms are not likely to leave us any time soon.

Clothing and cultural elements are changing, too, but the South maintains certain standards that exceed the rest. While it is true that there are plenty of silly sights to see at a Walmart in Olive Branch, Mississippi, I have seen plenty of folks in Northwestern Connecticut that could win a gold medal in a redneck competition. Meanwhile, Tuckahoe and Charleston still enjoy a class that is distinct from the Old Navy® model of cargo shorts and cheap sweatshirts. Seersucker suits, linens, and pastels speak to an elevated elite in the South. Girls simply do not go out in public without their hair and make-up. I can generally tell transplants from Southern females by the care or lack thereof regarding their appearance.

Beauty and social status are not feared in the South. No one looks down on a working man. Good Ole Boys, a distinct group of elites, and rednecks can be found discussing the weather over a beer or NASCAR at a cookout without a care for the other's "station." The girl from lower economic means will look just as pretty as her elite peers. We do not wear poverty as a source of shame. We wear poverty as a starting point, from which there is only one way to go – up, by the Grace of God.

As the Yankee-dominated leviathan attempts to root out our culture and make Dixie conform, it fails to overcome Southern idiosyncrasies born in our homes. Again, I return to the family and the woman that stands in the center of it. She feeds her family plates that are unique to the South. Yes, it is true, that generically "American" dishes have entered our homes. Our children love "dinosaur chicken," too. But they also love grits and eggs.

Bringing this altogether, one cannot see the South for what it is and will remain without having a full appreciation for the Southern woman. We wear make-up because we embrace the unique feminine appeal that is enjoyed by our sex. We do our hair for the same reason. It is a crown that frames our pretty faces. We have hips and we are not afraid to accentuate them with an apron. By definition, being a Southern woman is antagonistic toward modern definitions of feminism.

While modern feminists seek to dismantle so-called patriarchal distinctions of beauty, we own beauty. Being pretty is a treat to me and all of those around me. While modern feminists seek to break the division of labor, we embrace the functions of our female traditions. I love cooking and keeping a clean home. While modern feminists seek to replace men with women, we see men as our complementary partners who cannot be replaced – even when some of them are flawed. Let him fix the roof while I make supper.

How ironic that we now find ourselves as dissidents for promoting traditional values and morals. We have become dissidents for making biscuits and wearing pretty clothing. We are the rebels by refusing to shave our heads, pierce our noses, or take part in some form of physical debauchery. Yet here we are in modern times.

Thus, the humble, homemade biscuit becomes a weapon against progressivism. Teaching future generations how to make dishes from our soil versus purchasing mass processed ingredients is viewed with disdain. Why? Because they have no power over our kitchens. As I write this essay, the current president of these United States, Joe Biden, hopes to eliminate gas stoves. It is a pathetic attempt to exact control on that which happens within our homes. Like my grandmother and my great-grandmother, I intend to teach my children and grandchildren to keep resisting their attempts to control us, one recipe at a time.

Southern women have a responsibility to their people to form a wall that stops modernity from penetrating our homes and families. We do this out of love for our kith and kin. Like Sherman's invasion, this modern assault on our people seeks to destroy us. It seeks to force our surrender. We have a God given obligation to beat them by resisting. Southerners have been here before, except this time, we are poised to win.

The Southern woman helps win this war for the preservation of our culture and people by resilient resistance. She will put on her make-up. She will do her hair. She will don her apron. She will wear a dress. She will stand in her kitchen. She will teach her grandbabies how to make biscuits. The Southern woman will continue to feed her family – physically, emotionally, and spiritually – even after we win.

About the Author: Dixie O'Hara (pseudonym) is a Christian woman of Alabamian and Georgian stock. Her roots originate in Scotland, England, and Northern-Ireland, and her family settled in the South beginning at Jamestown, Virginia, in 1612. She is a wife and a mother to several beautiful daughters and three strong sons. Mrs. O'Hara began working in the food industry in 1993. She has been featured on television, runs a popular culinary blog, and she has published several cookbooks and articles under her real name. She resides in Georgia.

A Godly Endeavor: Worldview is Everything, *By Harry Bluff*

I: A Brief Explanation of Who We Are and of Our Aspirations

Were one to ask the pointed question "what is Southern Nationalism?" of any number of the authors of this work, one at a time and isolated from the rest, our inquisitor would likely receive as many slightly different definitions of the same as the number of respondents to whom he separately posed the question. Upon later examination (compare and contrast) of the various answers received, he would do well to avoid focusing on the slight differences in responses (not necessarily indication of disagreement in any case) and direct his focus instead on the broad and substantial concurrence among the whole concerning what it means to be a Southern Nationalist ("SN"), with goals and aspirations distinctive to Southern Nationalism. Presented with the question, this author's definition would read something like the following:

As a movement yet in its youth, the modern iteration of Southern Nationalism is fundamentally about working towards the permanent establishment of a separate and independent Southern nation on this continent; upon the soil bought and paid for by the blood, sweat, tears, and ceaseless toil of our noble ancestors during the span of more than four-hundred years; a nation "of, by, and for" true Southerners and Southern Nationalists. Plucking further from the annals of "great American literature" in giving definition to our aspirations, the end goal of the Southern Nationalist cause and mission is to [1] "secure the blessings of liberty to ourselves and our posterity." To our posterity, not to the world's posterity; and that through independent Southern nationhood – of the Southern people, by the Southern people, and for the Southern people.

As dedicated Southern Nationalists, we, the authors of the compilation of essays now before you, are devoted to the proposition of building a free and independent Southland: a new nation; a nation equipped to, and that therefore will, survive the test of time; a nation that will not collapse under attack from its avowed and mortal enemies, be they foreign or domestic. As such, ours is a monumental undertaking in its scope; its implications are staggering for mere mortal men and women to consider and to contemplate! It will require the coordinated and single-minded efforts of many thousands, nay, millions of devoted Southern patriots of both sexes, and covering a broad range of ages, talent pools and so forth, when all is said and done. This is to say nothing of the generous assistance and protective hand of Divine Providence that any endeavor of this importance and magnitude must always require to see it through to its happy conclusion (more on this below).

How far into the future we must look in anticipation of national freedom and independence is anyone's guess at this early date. We nevertheless strongly believe this can, and indeed that it must, be done. We further believe and assert that there is 'no time like the present' to begin a serious and formal discussion of the merits of that which we propose.

Of particular interest to readers generally no doubt, is the question of how we get from the ungrateful place in which we currently find ourselves - politically, socially, morally - to that date in the yet to be determined but hopeful future when our goal of forming a free, self-governing and independent Southern nation has been fully realized, and is an accomplished fact. Hence, Southern brothers and sisters, this collection of essays written and published for your serious and thoughtful consideration.

It is important to understand as well that, even should our worthy project ultimately fail or suffer the fate of yet another "lost cause," to be recorded in the annals of future history alongside that of our forefathers and mothers of '61-'65, those of us dedicated to the intoxicating prospect of Southern freedom and independence believe that we must at least try, for posterity's sake, if not for our own. The old adage has it that "if you ain't messing up, you ain't trying very hard." The authors concur with the spirit in which the adage was conceived and the message it is intended to convey. Namely, that any worthy endeavor is "risky business" by its very nature that will invariably involve lots of "mess-ups" along the way. But if we let fear of making mistakes dissuade us, nothing of real substance would ever get done. One thing is certain: failure is assured if we sit on our hands and do nothing; if we, moreover, do not take the next step in this important work as soon as humanly possible. Be it known that failure due to abdication of our responsibilities in this great and noble task is simply not an option among the able authors of these essays. If we go down, we'll go down fighting! But God helps them that help themselves, as another familiar adage so aptly states it.

To state our vision more succinctly, we Southern Nationalists strongly assert and affirm our inalienable right to self-determination and independent nationhood. This is not a question up for debate so far as we're concerned, any more than it was a question up for debate when America's Founding Fathers proclaimed it in their famous

Declaration of American Independence from the tyrannous rule of Mother England. One key to winning success in this worthy endeavor is that we, as a people, must be brought into, and kept within, the right spirit and the right frame of mind necessary to carry us through to its full and final achievement, or to our dying day, whichever comes first. This self-evident truth gives rise to a pointed discussion upon the importance of a common or shared worldview as essential to the success of our endeavors, start-to-finish. The remainder of this essay shall be dedicated to candidly discussing this vital aspect of our mission going forward.

II: Worldview Regarding the Success or Failure of Our Movement

The term worldview refers to that view of the world each individual embraces as his or her own, and thereby contributes to the general worldview of his or her people and nation. It is how he or she sees and understands the world (s)he lives in, his or her place in it, and therefore how (s)he conducts herself in all of her relations on a day-today basis. Boiled down, there are only two competing and opposing worldviews that we may correctly denominate for our purposes as follows: (1) Biblical-Christian; and (2) Secular-Pagan. By the previous statement it is simply meant that, of all the variations on worldviews represented throughout time and during the course of history, every one of these falls under the broader umbrella of one of the two above identified and respectively named. As Southern Nationalists solemnly devoted to the project of building a permanent free and independent Southland, the authors emphatically embrace and endorse the former of the two. But what does this mean; can Southerners reject or renounce the Biblical-Christian worldview and still be Southern Nationalists?

What it means, simply stated, is that we embrace a Biblical-Christian worldview, and therefore reject any variation of worldview not biblical and not explicitly Christian. Stated another way, we reject secular-paganism in all its varied forms; we declare the pagan worldview to be nothing less than the worship of idols and false gods (a violation of the 1st Commandment of the decalogue) and the propagation of false gospels, religious, and otherwise. As such, we consider the adoption by our people of alien worldviews and their principles detrimental to our goals, in direct proportion to the extent to which they embrace them. This means that we reject unbiblical (and extra-biblical) political and religious doctrines which propagate and teach a secular world and life view in competition with and in opposition to its superior bible-based counterpart.

There is a common saying among coaches of various sports: "we have to give ourselves a chance to win." What this means in relation to the importance of worldview to our movement, is that our designs would be doomed to fail from the outset were we to allow the principles of a secular or pagan worldview to influence our thinking and corrupt the movement. Of course, coaches can only do so much in giving their teams "a chance to win," they can call all the right plays at the exact right moments during the game, they can get their players set in the right defensive schemes etc., etc., but it is up to the players to execute when all is said and done. And this, again, illustrates why it is so important to a team's success to work under a unified team philosophy or worldview that all are, more or less, onboard with. The more onboard, the better, and the better chance of success.

As Southern Nationalists, we assert and affirm that the Holy Bible is the inerrant Word of God recorded for his peculiar people. That is to say, the book is His Word to and for Christians, through which He communicates with us, His people, and those who have been called by His name. We further assert and affirm that "All scripture is given by inspiration of God, and is profitable for doctrine, for reproof, for correction, for instruction in righteousness: That the man of God may be perfect, thoroughly furnished unto all good works." (2 Tim. 3:16)

We assert and affirm that among those good works knowledge of God's Word thoroughly furnishes His people to perform, is the good yet difficult works which must be done in preparing ourselves and our people as a people for separation and political independence from the degenerate, pagan nation and its citizenry commonly referred to as the United States of America. We firmly believe that the superstructure of a permanent, free and independent Southern nation must be erected upon the solid and immovable foundation of these great, immutable principles and truths.

The Biblical-Christian worldview further instructs its possessors to never become "unequally yoked together with unbelievers (2 Cor. 6:14)," nor to "cast your pearls before swine lest they turn again and rend you (Luke 7:6)," as has happened to the late, great United States. We strongly believe this timeless principle naturally extrapolates to application in the spheres of e.g., marriage and child-rearing, of education, to immigration and naturalization, and to the various branches of the entire political sphere.

The one true and living God - the God of the Bible - commanded our first parents in the Garden of Eden to "be fruitful and multiply," and to "replenish the earth and subdue it (Gn. 1:28)." We believe and assert that these principles also naturally extrapolate to supplying our national need for human laborers in various and sundry professions and vocations with the children of our youth. These children, Biblical-Christianity teaches, are to be faithfully reared and educated "in the way [they] should go," in the nurture and admonition of the Lord of hosts, that "when [they] are old, [they] will not depart from it (Pr. 22: 6)." This means that we assert and affirm our belief in, and undying commitment to, the biblical principle of lifelong marriage between one man and one woman (till death parts them), and of their having and raising and educating their own children, thereby supplying future generations of our Southern nation with Southerners, untainted by alien blood and uncorrupted by alien philosophies of God, man and government. Thereby shall we secure and perpetuate our national existence from generation to generation.

Our Lord and Savior taught us that to love God with all our heart, soul, mind and strength is the first and greatest of all the commandments, and that to love our neighbors as ourselves is like unto the first. "On these two commandments," our Savior further informs, "hang all the law and the prophets (Mark 12:30)." As Southern Nationalists who embrace the whole of the Bible and its teachings, we assert and affirm our commitment to these simple yet profound tenets of our faith. We further assert that self-love is natural and part of the human condition, whereas to truly love another "as thyself," one must come to know him or her in an intimate and meaningful way. This suggests that for mortal man to fulfill the dictates of the first and greatest commandment (supreme love to God), he must come to know the one true God and His nature, intimately and personally. This is primarily done through prayer (for wisdom and understanding) connected with personal Bible study, aided by a study of the early Church fathers, becoming familiar with systematic theology and orthodox Christian teaching: all faithfully passed down from generation to generation.

These form the basis of the methods by which we, as spiritual beings who are also flesh, gradually form a relationship with, and develop a deep and personal love for the great God of all creation, and thereby come to fully accept and internalize the Biblical-Christian world and life view, in all its parts and conditions, insofar as the limits of our individual understandings will allow. We strongly believe and assert that going to church once or twice a week is not sufficient toward developing a deep, personal and meaningful relationship with our Heavenly Father. We are commanded to love the Lord our God with all our minds and strength; with our intellects, in other words. This is why the intellectual exercise of studying "to show thyself approved unto God (2 Tim. 2:15)" is so important to the building of a deep and abiding reciprocal relationship with the Lord our God, and thereby develop an unshakable Biblical-Christian worldview, "ready always to give an answer to every man that asketh you a reason of the hope that is in you with meekness and fear (Rom. 6: 15)."

When our Savior answered the man to the effect above-cited, He was alluding to the two tablets of commandments given to Moses on Mt. Sinai; commandments 'written in stone' which our worldview teaches are ever-binding on us all. Upon the one were written those commandments directly pertaining to our (individual and collective) duty to the God of all creation; upon the second, those remaining six commandments directly related to our duty to our fellows. Thus, in answer to the scribe's query, our Lord narrowed the ten commandments of the decalogue to the two great commandments extracted from those tablets and to be inscribed on the hearts of His people - supreme love to God, and love towards our kith and kin. The world and life view all true and dedicated Southern Nationalists should adopt and internalize (to the fullest extent possible commensurate with his or her ability to understand its life-giving, life-sustaining principles) instructs to strictly obey God's holy commands contained in the decalogue and throughout the Holy Scriptures. We assert and affirm that disobedience to God and His commands is sin, simply stated; and we rest in the assurance of the scriptural admonition declaring that while "righteousness exalts a nation," serial disobedience and rebellion against God's holy commands is "a reproach to any people." (Pr. 14: 34)

III: Worldview as It Relates to Human Reason

A wise and learned American educator once opined of the human faculty of reason, that it is all too often a "miserable guide" to follow; one which "often errs from ignorance, and more often from the impulse of passion." [2] Our learned educator further explained that this notorious inability of the mass of human beings to reason correctly is generally attributable to two primary causes: to a lack of experience, and to a want of heavenly assistance via the free gift of divine revelation. We assert and acknowledge the truth of this great and timeless principle affirming the ever-present need of divine help each of us must receive from day to day in rightly exercising our God-given faculty of reason.

We further state that the great God of all creation has graciously furnished His faithful people with ample supplies of the raw materials necessary to honing our reasoning abilities and of learning to reason correctly with divine assistance. These inexhaustible stores of divine wisdom, our generous and loving God has graciously supplied us via revelation of both the general (Nature), and of the special (Bible) kinds. We roundly reject and pronounce to be heresy the unChristian belief in the sufficiency of human reason unaided by divine revelation; and we further declare that those who adopt and embrace this unbiblical belief are not without their supernatural instructor in any case. Namely, that old deluder, Satan.

IV: The Worldview of Matthew Fontaine Maury

"The Bible is true and science is true, and therefore each, if truly read, but proves the truth of the other. ... They are both true; and when your men of science, with vain and hasty conceit, announce the discovery of disagreement between them, rely upon it, the fault is not with the witness of His records, but with the worm who essays to interpret evidence which he does not understand."

– M F. Maury

The quotation heading this section of the essay was specifically chosen for its illustrative quality of demonstrating the kind of character a deeply internalized Biblical-Christian worldview cannot fail to produce in the hearts and minds of teachable men and women of God who imbibe its eternal principles. Maury, of course, was an extraordinary man who possessed extraordinary giftings and talents; and extraordinarily gifted and talented men can and often do achieve extraordinary things that the average person hasn't the capacity for achieving. However, it must be remembered as well that the Biblical-Christian worldview that manifests so vividly in virtually all of Maury's written works was no more natural to Matthew

Fontaine Maury than it is to most any other Southerner. Maury was blessed to have been born to godly Southern parents, who themselves were the products of Christian parents, and so on down the line. This brief sketch of Maury's family history serves to explain through whom, and at what juncture of his life, the seeds of the Biblical-Christian worldview so evident throughout Maury's writings in his manhood were planted in the fertile soil of his mind.

Maury's biographer was his daughter, Diana Fontaine Corbin. She wrote of her father's knowledge of God's Word in part that, [4] "Matthew's father was very exact in the religious training of his family… He would assemble them night and morning to read the Psalter for the day, verse and verse about; and in this way, so familiar did this barefooted boy become with the Psalms of David, that in afterlife he could cite a quotation, and give chapter and verse, as if he had the Bible open before him."

The quotation heading this section is an extract from the keynote address Maury gave at the laying of the cornerstone of The University of the South, now known as Sewanee University in East Tennessee. The important point to be gleaned from the excerpt is that the Biblical-Christian worldview does not deny the truths discovered through science; what it does deny, and emphatically so, is the lie of secularism stating that the Creator of the world and of all that therein is - the God of the Bible - is not the source and author of scientific truth, and that therefore there is no need to consult God's Word in confirmation of scientific truths or in discerning "scientific" falsehoods.

[5] Were there space enough left in my page allotment for this essay, I could quote extensively from Maury's writings in further confirmation of his having early received the seeds of, and having developed throughout his life, a strong and abiding Biblical-Christian worldview. Since there isn't room enough, the writer strongly urges readers to consult the sources listed in the citations, which

will, in turn, lead him or her to additional sources not listed here. In the meantime, imagine with me for a moment how very different the Southern nation would look and conduct herself were her people generally to embrace and imbibe the principles of a truly authentic Biblical-Christian world and life view such as Matthew Maury possessed and expressed during the entire course of his adult lifetime!

Many of the problems which afflict the Southern people at this date in time would, for all intents and purposes, disappear upon their collective internalization of the principles of the worldview in question: the bane of single-motherhood and illegitimate child bearing would all but cease to exist and afflict us; divorce would become such a rarity that our collective memory would soon forget the untold damage this pox on society does to families and to the nation as a whole; emasculated men would all but disappear from our nation; women, in general, would become more feminine, and the pox of militant feminism would be relegated to the fringes; deviant sexual lifestyles would be recognized by all as the Satanic manifestations they are, and would cease to be tolerated by a righteous people; Southerners, in general, would become more honest and kinder in their dealings with their Southern brothers and sisters, and their guests alike, etc. And most importantly of all, we as a nation and a people would win back God's approval and favor, and therefore receive His full blessing upon our endeavors. (2 Chr. 7:14)

V: Concluding Remarks

In conclusion, permit me to first say that I am honored and gratified that my humble submission has found its way into this little volume. My fondest hope is that you, dear reader, will seriously ponder the principles and the arguments as I've stated them throughout its several pages, and that you will glean some new and helpful insight or other therefrom. The work we are setting about to begin and see to its fulfillment is of vast importance to the future of the Southern people, and the author hopes and prays that he has at least provided you with certain "building blocks" for ideas of how best and most effectively to do your part in securing that future that you will soberly consider and ponder in the days and weeks and months ahead.

None of us possesses a perfectly honed Biblical-Christian world and life view, and certainly not this writer; there is always room for improvement, as they say. But one's worldview needn't be perfectly honed, and perfection isn't achievable in any case due to our sinful and imperfect nature, which always and inescapably causes us to err to some extent or other, regardless of how "honed" or developed one's worldview is at any given moment in time. The primary thing to understand is the importance of a correct worldview to our movement's viability start to finish, and therefore how to continually develop and hone a "more perfect" Biblical-Christian philosophy of life and living within your own heart and mind from this day forward, that you may pass down its timeless principles to your progeny in their youth, thereby doing your small but vital part in supplying the Southern nation with the next generations of God-fearing, God-honoring, Bible-believing Christian men and women who will perpetuate Southern freedom and national independence in the coming generations.

Thank you all for your time and consideration, dear readers. God bless you all, Southern brothers and sisters, and may God bless all of our honest and worthy endeavors, especially our work of building a future free and independent Southern nation, guided by the principles and influence of a strong and abiding Biblical-Christian worldview!

*****

Addendum I: A Note on Education

It is assumed that many, if not most, who will ultimately read these essays have children and/or grandchildren, as well as nieces and nephews of their own. It is also assumed that many, if not most, of those children and/or grandchildren, and nieces and nephews, attend public schools, and are therefore daily exposed to a steady diet and the corrupting influence of the secular-pagan worldview under which the government schools and their teachers and administrators generally operate, often unknowingly to themselves, but more often with a general attitude of indifference to the importance of worldview to true education.

Be it known that it is not the intention of the authors to accuse or insult those Southern parents and grandparents whose children attend public schools and who thereby receive a daily dose of secular-pagan instruction in those institutions. What this means, however, is that your task of instilling the seeds of the Biblical-Christian worldview in the hearts and minds of your children is made a great deal more difficult than it would or need be otherwise. We respectfully encourage those Southern parents and natural guardians of their children to prayerfully consider making other arrangements for their children's educations, whether it be homeschooling or private schooling.

Addendum II: Answer to an Anticipated Objection

It is not within the scope of this writing to anticipate and answer every objection that will eventually come down the pike. However, one anticipated objection seems important to address within the pages of this essay. Namely, the objection against time or timeframe.

It will be urged by some, perhaps by many, that we simply do not have time enough left before the impending collapse to convince Southerners to fully embrace and adopt a Biblical-Christian worldview, and that therefore this aspect of our work must not be made a priority at this critical date. I won't speak to the objection or its merits one way or the other, except to acknowledge that the concern against time is certainly real enough as best as I can tell. But there is also the greater reality that none of us is God, and therefore none of us knows how much time we actually have to achieve our goals no matter how clearly we think we see the proverbial "handwriting on the wall."

At the end of the day, it is the Sovereign God of the universe who will determine (who has in fact predetermined) how much time we have left. In the meantime, we must be about His work for our people; and preparing their minds and hearts to adopt and internalize a proper worldview that will buoy them up and sustain them through the struggles, the trials, the tribulations of becoming a truly free and independent people once again is, to the mind of this writer at least, a necessary prerequisite to attaining full, complete, and final victory.

About the Author: Harry Bluff (pseudonym) is a current officer in the United States Armed Forces. A graduate of one of the American military academies, Mr. Bluff is a frequent critic of the current state of new officers entering into the service. He has written his dissenting opinions using a number of pseudonyms designed to conceal his true identity, in hopes that the leadership of the modern Department of Defense would abandon the deleterious policies that cripple American military readiness. Now, recognizing that the US Armed Forces is set on a flank speed course of devastation beyond repair, he advocates for Southern secession. Mr. Bluff hopes a Free, Independent, and Godly Dixie will restore honor to the once proud military service within which he currently serves. Until then, he will continue to work with young officers of like mind to ensure something is left for their future.

Cousins? Distinctions between Southern Nationalism and White Nationalism, *By Neil Kumar*

Is Southern Nationalism the same thing as White Nationalism? The short answer is yes and no. This vexing topic is rarely if ever addressed, and the Southern cause is consequently reduced to a myopic, quaint subsidiary of a larger quest for a White ethnostate. Many racially conscious young Southerners, most of whom embrace their Southern identity, reflexively refer to themselves as "White Nationalists." This is, at least partially, because they see their own Southern identity as lesser than and subordinate to their White identity. If Southern Nationalism is ever to capture a critical mass of these young men, the already racially awakened, then it is incumbent upon us to explain why, far from being a narrow, curious sect of White Nationalism, Southern Nationalism becomes an entirely different entity.

First, we must acknowledge that the South is ethnically White. When we speak of the South, we speak of the White South. Conversations related to the South rarely involve the large population of black residents because they generally view themselves as distinct, despite their large (albeit minority) share of the population. Thus, the South as "White," is generally regarded by almost all parties and rarely involves considerations of other racial parties. This is not debatable. It is simply a fact, one which is so self-evident that it is often taken for granted. In this respect, it can unequivocally be stated that Southern Nationalism is necessarily White Nationalism, but that White Nationalism is *not* necessarily—and is indeed often directly at odds with—Southern Nationalism. We are White, but our racial identity does not, in and of itself, provide us with the nourishing fire which impels us forward. Our racial identity is a *component* of our primary, *Southern*, identity.

Our Christian identity is another component of our Southern identity. When we speak of the South, we not only mean the White South. We mean the White *Christian* South. Dixie is God's

Country, and we are God's people - perhaps not His only people, but His people indeed. In this respect, one could state that Southern Nationalism is necessarily Christian Nationalism, but of course, Christian Nationalism is not Southern Nationalism. Here, we have our first major divergence from White Nationalism.

Unfortunately, White Nationalism – as a movement – is afflicted with a deep antipathy for Christianity. To be sure, there is not much, if anything, about contemporary organized Christianity to recommend or endear itself to rightists of any stripe. Jesus Christ Himself would abhor much of what today passes for "Christianity." The subversion of Christianity, however pervasive, still cannot change the Word of God. Indeed, the grass withered, the flower fadeth, but the word of our God shall stand forever.

Large numbers of White Nationalists, perhaps even constituting a majority, have no interest in reading or otherwise learning this truth. Instead, they nonsensically slander Christianity as

"Jewish," which would be news to the Jews. For millennia, Judaism and Christianity were distinctly antagonistic toward one another. Regardless, White Nationalists often create absurd cults, adopt pagan practices centuries removed from an idealized, obscure pre-Christian past, or rely on cold, dispassionate scientism. While we do not view these misguided, lost souls as our adversaries, nor can they be viewed as our allies. We do not share any semblance of a common vision or mission with non-Christians.

Another major point of divergence for Southern Nationalists is that our cause is specific, while that of White Nationalists is abstract. Our goal, distilled to its purest, most essential form, is a Free and Independent Dixie, which one could see as a sort of reconstituted Confederate States of America. Our cause is rooted in one particular location – the South – and one particular people - White, Christian Southerners. Ours is an uncompromising and practically defined vision, one which is more feasible than that of the inherently vague White Nationalist ethnostate. For example, where should such a state be? Even this simple question proves unanswerable with any degree of satisfaction by any great number of self-identified White Nationalists.

Furthermore, our identity as Southern is specific, corresponding to a real, historically defined, culturally, linguistically, and politically distinct population. While anti-White leftists and egalitarian "colorblind" civic nationalists often make the ridiculous claim that White people do not exist (e.g., "I'm not White, I'm Italian"), while in the next breath uttering genocidal statements about those same White people whom they claim do not exist, there is a kernel of truth to the challenge.

Pan-European unity is a fiction; White people generally do not define their identities on purely racial grounds, but rather by their nationality. Far from joining hands as racial kinsmen, the kingdoms and then the nation-states of Europe have engaged in perpetual warfare against each other. When White men refer to themselves as such, their nationality subordinated to their race, it is typically limited to situations of oppositional ethnogenesis, where an external racial threat is involved - such as Amerindians, blacks, etc. And yet, even then, these expressions of White identity are often still expressions of national identity, the nation itself understood to consist of White people, rather than a conceptually White nation.

It is certainly true, for all intents and purposes, that America was intended to be and did function as a White nation for most of its history. Until the 1965 Hart-Celler Immigration Act, America boasted a 90% White supermajority and a small black minority, with other racial groups demographically insignificant – though not politically insignificant. But, while American men always saw and referred to themselves as White, it is only after the triumvirate of desegregation, the 1964 Civil Rights Act, and the 1965 Immigration Act that White Nationalism began to emerge.

Before the middle of the twentieth century, White identity was merely a component of, and thus subordinate to, American identity. But American nationalism itself was an invention of war propaganda, most clearly traceable in its contemporary iteration to the bloodthirsty tyrant Abraham Lincoln's Gettysburg Address. Without delving too deeply into the historical thicket, it will suffice to say that White Nationalism is a thoroughly modern creation.

Southern Nationalism, by contrast, is premised upon a Southern identity forged by centuries of blood, fire, and siege. Southern identity predates any American identity, and, while Southern men did see themselves and refer to themselves as White, their sectional identity as Southerners was always first. This identity was so deeply ingrained in the Southern psyche that it survived well after desegregation. Indeed, even today, large numbers of Southerners, perhaps even constituting a majority, still see themselves as Southern, although this has become subordinated both to American and partisan political identities (i.e., "red state" Republicans). Southern

Nationalism emerged in the antebellum period, mere decades before the War for Southern Independence, primarily in response to Northern rhetorical vitriol, political animus, and economic aggression. But its antecedent, Southern sectionalism, predated even the American War of Independence.

Summarizing their origins, White Nationalism was a response to a sudden political and societal shift in the mid-to-late 1960s. Southern Nationalism was an organic growth born out of a shared history, culture, religious, and ethnic construct, emerging out of early American sectionalism and solidifying during the antebellum period. That stated, the two share some challenges.

For reasons related likely to competition, globalist elites in the United States have decided that White people, and especially Southerners, are no longer welcome in the future of a new world order. However, their definition of "White" is more closely related to the same definition both White and Southern Nationalists share than the definition of "White" in the Civic Nationalist context. By "White," these globalist elites exclude the Jewish people. In large part, despite their relatively small proportion of the population, the vast majority of these same globalist elites enjoy a Jewish heritage – thus, the exclusion. Consequently, their focus is on the eradication of White Christians in the United States and other areas of the West, not simply those who have a Caucasian skin tone. This assertion is reinforced by the thousands of articles and statements made by globalist elites – from academia to entertainment – celebrating the destruction of "Whiteness" or attacking White societies.

Targeting Whites for elimination or proportional reduction comes with it a targeting of functional Eurocentric societies. Thus, it is not enough to simply "replace" the race in their respective homelands – including the United States. Rather, they often profane the sacred through deleterious social programming and an inversion of normative behavior. The sicker, the filthier, the fouler, the better. Nonwhites, including American blacks and the constellation of "refugees" and "migrants" from Africa, Asia, the Middle East, and Central and South America, are then exploited as shock troops in a hyper-democratized state. By depicting Whites as "the enemy" and White society as "systemically racist" or antithetical to their racial/ethnic make-up, disaffected minorities vote to remove the very systems of governance within which they thrive at the behest of politically manipulative globalist elites.

The result is one in which Southern Nationalists and White Nationalists find common cause for defense, even if their ultimate solutions differ. The two find their proverbial backs against a wall, forced to fight in a shared cause of survival. Furthermore, they also immediately recognize the destructive impact of globalist elites on their previously, highly functioning societies. Suddenly, policy changes created by the same globalist elites and empowered by leftist voting blocs comprised of minority communities lead to sharp crime surges, a reduction in nominal earnings, and the elimination of jobs, while drug addictions and suicide rates rise. To save a functional world order, the distinct Nationalist camps often recognize the true origins of the problem and that is where messaging and strategies often complement or intersect.

But this is not the end of the story for Southern Nationalists. No, the Southern people have an additional adversary, one who has inflicted far greater material and psychic damage upon Dixie than globalist elites ever have: the Yankee. Northern Whites have been, and arguably still are, our most pernicious foes. While it is true that all Whites are under attack from a truly genocidal force, Southerners face a deeper hatred than any other White ethnic group - save perhaps Russians - including from fellow Whites. Indeed, many prominent White Nationalists today heap scorn upon the South and our Confederate heritage.

The Yankees literally put Dixie to the torch and the sword in the War for Southern Independence and then enslaved her in the most humiliating fashion conceivable during

Reconstruction. Federal soldiers committed atrocities against Southern civilians at an unprecedented scale, the first real example of total warfare waged by a nominally civilized power. The next example would be the Anglo-Boer War, to which historians have devoted far more sympathy.

After the Yankees razed and materially annihilated the South, they subjected her to a decade of black political domination, during which the same White Northerners squeezed every last drop of blood from the already despoiled Southern turnip. The descendants of these carpetbaggers wreak the same havoc across the South today. They occupy our hometowns and our wildernesses, emanating as locusts from the coasts. They have already destroyed in order to devour our birthrights in a grand scheme of physical, economic, political, and cultural dispossession.

What is now happening to the White race writ large is the globally recognized definition of the term "genocide." It was tragically initiated in the South long ago. We were the canaries in the coalmine, yet nobody cared. Indeed, many Whites – including self-identified "patriotic, conservative" Whites – enthusiastically cheered, led, and/or participated directly in the defenestration of Dixie. Our Southern forebears clearly saw the true nature of the United States government more than a century before the contemporary Right did: a monstrous Federal Leviathan. Again, nobody cared.

Here, we come to another major point of divergence. Generally speaking, White Nationalists envision a single ethnostate or multiple ethnostates functioning as a White homeland, along the lines of: (1) some reclamation of the entire landmass of these United States of America as the nominally singular polity it now purports to be or (2) a combination of balkanized ethnostates operating as a loose confederacy. Complicating this picture is the attachment of some American White Nationalist intellectuals to the concept a pan-European supranational project, something akin to a racially conscious European Union.

Southern Nationalists start from the premise that these United States of America as a political unit is dead and has been since 1860. The quintessentially American spirit that animated our ancestors in 1776 and 1861 was slaughtered on the battlefield in 1865. We do not put "America" first, because America does not exist. We are *Dixie* first. Even if it were feasible to reclaim the entire landmass of the currently extant United States - and it most certainly is not - we have no desire to do so. We do not give one hoot about the fate of New York, California, Illinois, Ohio, or any other state not represented by the thirteen stars on each of the national flags of the Confederate States of America. While the Southern Nationalist project involves a sort of balkanization of the currently extant United States, the prevailing locations contemplated by White Nationalists for their ethnostate invariably exclude the South. Many White Nationalists have even suggested giving large swathes of the South to black people.

In Dixie's land, we'll take our stand. The South is nonnegotiable. We place no stock in a vague, abstract "homeland" dominated by deracinated Yankees. Our homeland has a single location. Southern identity, although inherently racially defined by White identity, is simultaneously deeper, narrower, and yet more expansive than bare White identity. My own heritage is instructive of the difference between Southern identity and White identity.

I am half-White and half-Indian. My maternal lineage is Scots-Irish. It's through this side of my ancestry that I am a proud member of both the Sons of the American Revolution and the Sons of Confederate Veterans. My earliest ancestors in this line emigrated to the Colonial South in the mid-to-late seventeenth century, perhaps even as early as Jamestown in 1616.

I have at least two ancestors who served South Carolina in the American War of Independence. Glass Caston, my fifth-great grandfather, was born in 1732 in Essex County,

Virginia, and became a carpenter and wheelwright. In 1754, he bought land in Orange County, North Carolina, where he quickly got involved in local politics, becoming constable in 1756. In 1763, Glass bought land in Craven County, in what is now Lancaster County, South Carolina. In 1765, he was appointed one of the County's Justices. During our War of Independence, Glass served as Wagon Master for a supply train in Colonel Kershaw's Regiment, supplying patriots stationed at Purrysburg, near Savannah. After the War, Glass continued in public service; in 1784, he even ran against General Thomas Sumter, the "Fighting Gamecock," for a seat in the State Assembly. He passed away in 1804.

Captain John Blakeney, my sixth-great-grandfather, was also born in 1732, in Mount Blakeney, Limerick County, Ireland. John came to the colonies around 1750, and by the early 1760s had settled in Chesterfield County, South Carolina. He became a substantial landowner and a successful planter. In 1775, he was elected captain of the local militia. The next year, he received a captain's commission from the Provincial Congress and raised a regiment. John and his men were assigned to Colonel Benton's Regiment, where he served as a sergeant under the "Swamp Fox," General Francis Marion. John passed away in 1832, at the age of 100.

I have at least eight ancestors who served the Confederacy in the War for Southern Independence. Newman Robinson, my second-great grandfather, was born in 1841. He enlisted in the Confederate Army on April 8, 1861, just a few days before the Battle of Fort Sumter. He served throughout the War in the 5th Regiment of the South Carolina Volunteers, known as the Lancaster Greys. He was discharged from service a full four years after he had enlisted, on April 9, 1865, when General Lee surrendered at Appomattox. He passed away in 1924.

Newman's father, Phillip, my third-great grandfather, served in the same company with him. Philip, born around 1815, was a plantation overseer.

He was probably killed during the War. Newman's brother, Warren, born in 1842, also served with the Lancaster Greys during the War. He passed away in 1916.

Lewis Rowell, another of my second-great grandfathers, was born in 1846. At age 16, he and his father, Henry, both enlisted in the Confederate Army, serving through the end of the War. At his death on June 15, 1944, at age 98, Lewis was the last surviving veteran of the War for Southern Independence in Lancaster County, South Carolina. On special occasions, like church service, Lewis wore his trademark white homespun suit. His birthday parties were the biggest event in the community each year, always attended by three to five hundred people.

My third-great grandfather, Jeff Ellis, was a Corporal in the 12th Regiment of the South Carolina Infantry. He was wounded at Manassas in 1862, and again at Wilderness. In 1870, he passed away as the result of complications from those wounds.

My paternal line, as you likely surmised from my last name, is North Indian. Unfortunately, I don't have as detailed knowledge of this side of my lineage. My grandfather, long since passed, was the genealogist of his family, and apparently took this knowledge with him to the grave.

My father came to North Carolina from India in 1984, joining several of his older brothers who had moved here before him. Interestingly, he had been reluctant to come to America. But his brothers asked him to join them, so he did. In India, he had been involved with the Rashtriya Swayamsevak Sangh (RSS), a Hindu nationalist paramilitary organization which serves as the backbone of the Indian Right. The RSS is closely tied to the current (at the time of this writing) BJP government. He waited until 2001 to become a citizen, not wanting to officially sever ties with his homeland. If it weren't for my mother, he may well have returned to India in the 1980s.

Growing up mixed-race was interesting. In many ways, I had a traditional Southern upbringing.

In other ways, I had a cosmopolitan upbringing. My parents loved to travel, and being an only child, I always went with them. I've now visited nearly thirty countries on four continents.

My mom is a Southern Baptist, my dad a Hindu, but I was raised a Southern Baptist. All of my friends are White. I never learned how to speak Hindi. I never identified as anything other than American. Beginning around junior high and high school, though, I began to experience identity issues. By "identity issues," I mean that I suddenly had a hard time fitting in and feeling a sense of belonging; part of this likely stemmed from being an only child, but I suspect that it was also at least partially driven by the fact that I had two cultures, two ancestries within me.

As I began to experience the alienation common to modern adolescence, I rebelled against my Southern roots and my Christianity. In this rebellion, I turned not towards my Indian heritage, but rather towards deracinated urban liberalism. I found my way home again, but I went through Hell to find my way back.

What had started as experimentation in high school developed into full-blown drug and alcohol addiction through most of my years at the University of Chicago. You name the drug, and I've almost certainly done it. You wouldn't believe me if I told you how much liquor I drank on a daily basis, the copious quantities of hard drugs I did almost every night. I am blessed to still be alive. By the Grace of God alone, I overcame my addictions cold turkey. I've been fully sober now for four years.

My time at the University of Chicago also coincided with my awakening. Growing up in 90% White Bentonville, Arkansas, I bought the egalitarian hogwash hook, line, and sinker. It wasn't until I moved to Hyde Park, on the South Side of Chicago, that this veil was pierced. There, I witnessed racial reality for the first time - this was the first time that I had really had any dealings with urban blacks. It was also my first interaction with

Jewish people, as well as many other ethnic minorities.

While I noted that there were no Southerners among the students or faculty, I found it strange that such a vast majority of faculty members were Jewish despite the fact that they comprise a tiny minority of the American population. Ironically to me at the time, the majority of students in many of my courses were Jewish. I even had at least one Jewish roommate for most of my first two years. I learned a lot about the culture through interaction.

My racial awakening coincided with the 2016 election. Seeing every single center of institutional power on earth align to destroy the Trump campaign really opened my eyes. Donald Trump was a totally non-ideological, pragmatic civic nationalist whose only real offense was speaking about issues that adversely affect Whites. He articulated the genuine concerns of average White people. I'm under no illusions about Trump or his failed presidency, but his election was epochal; for the first time in many years, Whites began to feel that they had a voice. That was Trump's crime.

I started systematically re-educating myself. Kevin MacDonald's *Culture of Critique* is certainly the book most formative in my understanding of globalist power dynamics. But it was Richard Weaver's *The Southern Tradition at Bay* and Eugene Genovese's *The Mind of the Master Class*, combined with Shelby Foote's *The Civil War*, that set my long-dormant Southern blood ablaze. You see, it was not until I understood the truth about the South that I was able to understand the other truths that I have since come to learn.

I read hundreds of books in a three-year period, from 2016 through 2019. Of course, I haven't stopped. The point is that I returned home, both spiritually and physically, and reinforced that return home intellectually and emotionally.

I read the entire King James Bible, for the first time in my life. I was saved, and then baptized. I gained a passion for my family history, my

Southern ancestry, and joined SAR and SCV. I found my calling, my purpose, the reason for which God placed me on this earth at this time: to protect, fight for, and advance the interests of my people, the Southern people.

I'm not ashamed in the slightest of my Indian ancestry. I love and embrace all of my family, and of course I feel a kinship with India. It is only natural that I do. But I do not situate my identity nor my loyalty there. Though I am mixed-race, I am not mixed-identity. I am not an American, or an Indian. I am a Southron.

To those who believe that our day is done, that our cause is lost, I say: you know what they say about Southerners and Lost Causes. Our forefathers left their homes and their beloved behind, risking everything, laying down their lives and charging so bravely into the mouth of Hell because they knew that if they did not fight, their homeland would be lost. It would be transformed into their worst nightmares.

They gave everything they possessed in order to transmit their inheritance, their Southern birthright, to generations yet unborn. They knew, if they stood by, their entire world would end. They intrinsically understood that the world which they built for their children would be stolen from them and divvied into the hands of squatters not fit for the blessings of their civilization.

Pickett's Charge, bloody as it was, should be the image etched in our hearts, the pool from which we draw our fortitude. These Southern heroes, common men only months before, fearlessly stormed an unassailable position, marching headlong into the impenetrable Yankee Leviathan because it was their duty. Union Colonel Frank Haskell described the Confederates thusly:

> *None on that crest now need be told that the enemy is advancing. Every eye could see his legions, an overwhelming, resistless tide of an ocean of armed men sweeping upon us! ...Right on they move, as with one soul, in perfect order, without impediment of ditch, or wall, or stream, over ridge and slope,*

through orchard, and meadow, and cornfield, magnificent, grim, irresistible.

Let not our enemies need be told that *we* are advancing, immovable, magnificent, grim, irresistible.

We should also consider Edmund Ruffin, the greatest Fire-Eater of them all, a gentleman who spent most of his adult life laying the discursive groundwork for secession. At age 67, he fired the very first shot on Fort Sumter from Morris Island. After Lee's surrender at Appomattox, Ruffin chose to commit suicide rather than submit to Yankee rule, writing his famous last words:

> *And now, with my latest writing and utterance, and with what will [be] near to my latest breath, I here repeat, and would willingly proclaim, my unmitigated hatred to Yankee rule — to all political, social, and business connection with Yankees, and to the perfidious, malignant, and vile Yankee race.*

It should go without saying that I am not advocating for Ruffin's final course of action. But we should embody the principle: that, if we fail, life is not worth living. We have to understand this: everything that we love and cherish about our country, all that is pure and good on this earth, is directly tied to the reclamation of our Southern nation.

Remember, and never forget, what we are fighting for. *The Andy Griffith Show* has always been one of my favorite programs. Mayberry, North Carolina, the fictional town that it was set in, is a perfect image of midcentury Southern life. Our enemies tell us that Mayberry never existed. They're wrong. Hundreds, if not thousands, of "Mayberrys" existed all over the South. My mom was blessed to have grown up in one.

My mother grew up in a tiny little town called Rich Hill, South Carolina. Her father was a sharecropper, and her mother was a homemaker. My mom lived next door to her grandparents, and every Sunday, after church, most of the extended family - more than fifty people - would gather there for a supper of fried chicken fresh from the coop, homemade biscuits, fresh vegetables, home churned butter, chess pie, pound cake, chocolate pie, and so forth. On hot summer days, they'd sit under the oak tree churning ice cream.

Every year, her grandfather planted a garden, plowing it with a mule, walking behind in his worn leather brogans with this old iron plow. My mom would help the family shuck corn, hull peas, and string green beans. There was a lot of vegetable canning. They washed their clothes by hand.

After school, my mother would run next door and climb onto her grandpa's lap under that oak tree. She'd reach in his pocket, and he always had a piece of gum or penny candy for her. Every day, he'd walk up the road to the corner store to visit with his friends and get his grandkids a treat. Her grandmother was always reading the Bible, rocking on the front porch.

That's what we're fighting for. Our posterity. A future for our children, a world in which that communitarian ideal isn't just a memory, but a reality.

The blood of heroes courses through our veins. Through this ancestral blood, our forefathers commune with us. Their blood - *our* blood - calls out to us, challenges us, exhorts us, asking us why we allowed our enemies to drag us to this sordid, miasmic state of decay, *commanding* us to fight and to secure victory - not just to secure our existence and our future, but to *triumph* and fulfill the glorious plans they laid for us - to realize the future which they made possible for us.

Our duty is to take up our ancestors' mantle, to preserve the birthright for which they sacrificed everything to bequeath to us, to stop squandering our inheritance and instead *make ourselves worthy of their blood.*

Our duty is to fill our descendants' hearts with the admiration for us that we have for our forefathers, to give our children, our grandchildren, our great-grandchildren, and their children after them a legacy to uphold, a name to honor, a *kingdom* to maintain and advance.

It will take everything that we have and all that we are, but we can and will reclaim our homeland. It is ours, and ours alone. It belongs to nobody else, and it never will. What other region of the raped and desecrated corpse that is the United States of Weimerika has managed to hold on to any semblance of an identity?

I am a Southern Nationalist. The South lives yet. The South shall survive, or we shall die with her. And as ever, the Lord will vindicate our blood.

About the Author: Neil Robinson Kumar ran for U.S. Congress in Arkansas's Third District in 2022, representing six Ozark counties. He received nearly 17,000 votes, amounting to almost a quarter of the total, against a six-term neocon incumbent with unlimited money in the home of Walmart.

He is a graduate of the University of Chicago and is now in his final year at the University of Arkansas School of Law. A member of both the Sons of the American Revolution and the Sons of Confederate Veterans, his lineage can be traced to Jamestown. His work has been featured at the Abbeville Institute, American Renaissance, Counter-Currents, Identity Dixie, The Occidental Observer and Quarterly, Clyde Wilson's Reckonin', VDARE, and the Unz Review, among others. His next book is a history of the Reconstruction Ku Klux Movement.

Become Mythical, Southern Man, *By Father O'Dabney*

The purpose of this book is to recapture the definition and very narrative of Southern Nationalism. Our quest for sovereignty began centuries in the past. The drive to explore, to build, and establish orderly societies is inherent in our Anglo-Saxon/Celtic blood. We have produced many of the greatest figures in Western Civilization. Warriors and explorers, theologians and philosophers, poets and playwrights, kings and queens, inventors, and architects… there has been no limit to what our people can achieve. We remember legendary figures such as Washington, Jefferson, Lee, Madison, Calhoun, Andrew Jackson, Forrest, "Stonewall" Jackson, ad infinitum. Their deeds are mythological. However, without rapid action on our part, their exploits, the very civilization they created will be lost, the South will be part of the greater devolving of our world, and barbarism will be its end. So, what can we do?

My task, in the smaller picture, is to help each of you see yourself in the current and future mythology of our people. To take that step into legend. To not just admire the greatest of our ancestors, but to inspire you into that greatness. It seems a rather large, even silly presumption to think of oneself as great. Our Southern humility forbids us even the notion, and that is exactly how greatness is born, in humility. Beginning with initial doubt – "I cannot change anything" – and then stepping forward and launching yourself into those unknown waters takes great courage. Yet, our ancestors, Southerners in general, are not disposed to others telling them what they can or cannot do. It gets our Irish up!

That agitation was the catalyst that moved my conscience in defiance. It compelled me to pick up my pen in obstinacy to an abusive empire. Ultimately, it led me to imagine myself and others in a prophetic vision of what must come, requiring a forward-looking mythology. We must be part of an origin story for a new Southern Nationalism. I began to see myself in the story, not just as an observer of history, but a participant. I suppose most legendary participants in history had no idea where Providence would lead them. They just started where they were and kept moving forward. We must do the same.

The story I chose to introduce this new mythology was the "Keeper of the Fire." It is the story of a man named Gideon, who is mysteriously thrust into action by a haunting figure, a guardian of our Southern people. His actions over decades of hard work leads to the eventual sovereignty of our people. The last part of that story is his funeral. Having finished his course, he is laid to rest by all the unexpected heroes birthed along the way. Below is that final chapter. It is my hope, my prayer, that you will see yourself in such a saga, and work to free our people.

Thus, my essay is not one that is driven by a logical series of arguments as those presented by my esteemed colleagues. Rather, I chose to introduce to you – the reader – a legend that can be.

It is fictional, for now. Many of the elements in the story you are about to read are in the works as you read this passage. They are taken from things that are happening today, caused by men who have surrendered everything for a cause bigger than themselves. I want you to understand that you can be part of this verbal imagery, too. I want the reader to know that this legend is becoming a reality and you can engrave your name within the passages of an eternal journey.

KNIGHT PASSES, Gideon Enters Mythology

My mother loved her father dearly, and so she was always reserved in disclosing information about him. She kept many things just for herself, not hidden from examination, but rather waiting for just the right moment to pull back the veil and reveal a world that could only be understood when the tapestry of events was collected and finished. Today was that day.

The night had passed, and the morning was grey and solemn. Misty was the air as the sun began to rise. Nothing unexpected had taken place. My grandfather was very old. He was the oldest of those that would gather here today. Each man had played his part over the years. Now, they all assembled. They were here to keep the promise, remembering their oath, and fulfilling the covenant that had given all of them strength in the troubled times.

Hidden amongst an ancient forest of oak trees, Spanish moss hanging low upon them, was a stone chapel. Four stone pathways led to another that encircled this sacred ground. By design, it was set off the road at some distance, only to be approached on foot, as to give those assembling time to prepare their hearts before entering this holy place. From the pathway to the south, you could hear the pipers playing the hallowed tunes of our people, low and mournfully.

Without rehearsal, one hundred and forty-three men, their eyes focused, swords at their sides, uniformed in black, Argyle jackets, tartan kilts woven with threads of grey, light blue, crimson, and golden maze, silently made their way toward two large wooden doors at the entrance of the chapel. Carved on one door was the bloom of the magnolia, the flower of our beloved homeland, and on the other, the bloom of the dogwood, the symbol of our crucified and risen Lord. On the floor of the narthex was a brilliantly and devilishly painted dragon, and every soul was commanded to stomp on its head upon entry, symbolizing eternal victory over our enemies and the enemies of our Lord.

After entering the chapel, eleven of the knights broke away to attend to other duties to which I was not privy. Only those of the knightly order had ever seen the inside of the chapel until this moment. As I was privileged to be his grandson, I was one of the first allowed to enter, though behind the rest of his children and my grandmother. Not until some time had passed were the rest of the mourners allowed to follow.

It was still cloudy outside, so the inside of the chapel was dark, the only light being from torches and candles. Yet, I could tell that it had been well crafted with a different assortment of wood and stone that are native to all the lands that now make up our homeland. Cedar, cypress, pine, oak, ash, and cherry fragrantly and beautifully made up a cornucopia of smells and sights that was other-worldly, like nothing my senses had ever experienced. I paused in distraction until my younger sister nudged me to my seat.

When everyone had entered and been seated, the doors to the chapel were shut hard, and the sound was as if thunder had clapped inside and bounced off the wood and stone. Then silence. It became so quiet that you could hear the person next to you breathe. I waited in anticipation, not knowing what would happen next. Excited and frightened, I looked to my mother and grandmother for comfort, but they were emotionless behind veils of black lace.

A knight from an elevated pulpit heralded all to rise and keep silent. One hundred and thirty of the knights moved into their positions; fifty in the balcony, forty along the back near the covered stained-glass windows, four sets of ten took up positions in the aisles aligned to form Saint Andrew's Cross. Suddenly, there was a loud knock at the doors from which we had all entered.

Once again, and with a deep and deliberate voice, the herald commanded the knight that had sealed and guarded the entrance to open the doors. And as he did, sunlight briefly entered the chapel. All heads turned toward the entrance, and all eyes beheld the eleven knights that had been missing.

"Who wishes to enter this sacred place!" boomed the herald.

In response, the lead knight soberly stated, *"We are Knights of the Southland."*

"And why have you come to this hallowed place?" the herald demanded.

"Our brother has fallen, and we have brought him home."

At that, the herald motioned them to enter.

You could hear the women start to weep as the procession entered. Five of the knights, three in the front and two in the back, held long pikes, at each step they struck the stone floors, paused, and crisply snapped their boots together. I have never heard a more solemn and intentional sound. Carried by the remainder of the eleven was the coffin that contained the mortal remains of my grandfather, a simple wooden coffin, brass handles, and draped in the once outlawed, but now celebrated, flag of our people.

My heart pounded, I watched the gathered knights as they unfurled all the flags of our new confederation, the banners of all the different orders represented, and the ancient flags of our ancestors from across the ocean. It was emotional, but it was more than that. It was regal, befitting nobility, and it was for a man that was as common as his Southern drawl. Or so I thought…

The honor guard carrying my grandfather's coffin continued toward the center of the chapel. The simple things he had taught me through conversations and games started to flood my mind. I could almost predict the rituals that would happen next, and though I had never been here nor seen anything like that which was before my eyes, it was all familiar.

The coffin was respectfully placed on a large granite table with the flag still draped over it. The table was eight feet long, four feet wide, with a depth of ten inches. Engraved around the edges were the last words of one of the saints of our people. "Let us cross over the river, and rest beneath the shade of the trees."

My memory was triggered. The images and sounds of the men who had visited my grandfather flashed and echoed. This saying was the way in which they had always parted from each other, almost in benediction, as if something sacred had taken place. That's how he was, every interaction was deliberate and purposeful, and all the more hurried as he got older.

At the time of his parting, he and his bride had been married 75 years. They had seven children, and to date 35 grandchildren, 27 great grandchildren, and six great, great grandchildren. All save two were present, two children already proceeding into eternal glory. Each of them had a personal story to be shared of him, but this was not the time.

Hymns and readings of selected Scripture, and quotes from some of the heroes of our people was the body of the service. There was no eulogy in the traditional sense. There was no unscripted emotional rambling so common at many modern funerals. There was no giddy celebration of life. This was a time to mourn. Those assembled had lost something of value, someone precious to them. It was my grandmother who had lost the most. So, it was left to her to choose who would take up the mantle and join the Circle of the Twelve, for there were always to be twelve.

Early on, during the restoration, within the ranks of the brotherhood, it was determined that the inner circle would represent families, avoiding infiltration and treachery. Therefore, each of the twelve would recruit from within their close familial relationships. Brothers, sons, sons-in-law, and close cousins would become the collective of one hundred and forty-four, and there was a general campaign to have all these families intermarry, solidifying the bonds even more. In the past, the power of real *connectionalism* had always been the strength of our people, and my grandfather worked tirelessly to reclaim this ancient power.

The herald called for my grandmother to pick from within her clan a replacement for my grandfather, completing the twelve. She called the name of her eldest son; he was the knight that had been guarding the entrance. He was the last of her sons to join the brotherhood, but once awakened, his strength and nobility was apparent to all. Stepping forward, he presented himself before the eleven, bowing down at the front of the table in respect and homage for that which he was being called.

"Are there any objections to our brother taking the sacred vows of our order?" the herald questioned the assembled knights. The chapel was silent in agreement to this choice. Then the herald asked my uncle if he was worthy to take the oath. He exclaimed *"No!"* This was the proper response,

for a knight must act in humility before all, knowing the heaviness of the duty for which he was about to embrace. Therefore, the ritual proceeded.

The herald asked him to repeat a series of vows before all those assembled and requested that none of these vows were to be repeated outside this sacred place. He did this soberly, as he was not only entering into the Circle of the Twelve, but he was acknowledging his patriarchal headship over his clan. Upon this acceptance, the oldest knight walked toward my uncle, drew his sword and knighted him in the name of Saint Andrew, and by the covenant of the Father, Son, and Holy Ghost. He rose and joined the circle to complete the twelve.

Now with the compliment of twelve restored, they encircled the table, swords drawn and raised over the coffin. Suddenly, all one hundred and forty-three knights proclaimed in deafening unison, *"Deo Vindice!"* ("With God as Our Defender") and the curtains that had hidden the stained-glass windows in the balcony were flung open, illuminating the chapel in radiant sunlight for the first time. Then, the windows in the lower chapel were uncovered, and the brilliance of every detail of the chapel was magnified! The sight amplified the emotions to a battle fervor among the knights. The herald loudly imparted another translation of the same expression, *"God is our Vindicator!"* At this, all the knights made their way quickly into the aisles on the main floor of the chapel and assembled by order and by clan.

Precisely at that moment, the questions my grandfather would repeatedly ask came rushing to my recollection, *"Who will defend our family?"* and *"How will your accusers be answered when they revile you falsely?"* The answer was always the same, *Deo Vindice! Deo Vindice! Deo Vindice*! For a moment, I forgot I was at a funeral and wanted to leave my seat, joining the rally of knights surrounding my grandfather, but that changed quickly.

All the knights turned toward my grandmother in respect, but also in truest love, for she was most beloved among them all. One by one, they all began to slowly sing our beautiful anthem, the anthem of our people. Their voices, gentle yet manly, like a cascade of rain falling inside the chapel. My grandmother, who had been stoic until this point, could no longer contain herself, and her grief finally befell her.

The flag draped coffin was now attended to once again, as the guard respectfully and precisely folded our glorious banner. The newest of the twelve was given the honor of presenting our flag, which was to be received by my grandmother. Only the knights were not overcome with emotion at this point, though looking toward my uncles, three of the knights' eyes were watering.

The doors of the chapel were opened once again. All were asked to rise as the coffin was again moved, but this time by the whole of the twelve. They raised it high above them and proceeded to exit. The rest of the congregation followed, each according to their clans, each attended to by the knights that represented them within the brotherhood. And as they left, they all sang, "The

Son of God goes forth to War," which was among the favorite hymns of my grandfather.

On the Southern side of the chapel was the tomb in which my grandfather would finally be laid to rest. The coffin was lowered and covered in Carolina jasmine, yellow and beautiful like a South Carolina morning sunrise. My grandmother, along with all her children, touched the coffin one last time, then it was placed and sealed within the tomb. It was finished, or so I thought…

It was December 20th, 200 years to the day that our beloved South Carolina had taken a stand against tyranny. How appropriate that my grandfather was laid to rest on this day, as the work of our ancestors was almost complete. The ceremonies of the day and all those gathered to honor him were dedicated to something much grander than themselves. They had kept the fire started so long ago, and it had proven to be unquenchable.

After the events of the day, I was exhausted on every level. My spirit had been low, raised to euphoria, then low again as his coffin was placed inside the tomb and sealed. Sensitive to my state, my grandmother sought me out. Even though she had been very busy in her hospitality, this genteel Southern lady instinctively knew I needed her, I needed her to bring me to a place of solace. Her gentle voice reminded me of where my grandfather would go to seek such a rest. After her calming words, I determined myself to head for the woods, at a campsite he had so frequently brought me.

Although the day had been perfectly pleasant, cooler weather was settling in, and a very rare and light snow was beginning to fall. Per her permission, I took my grandfather's old pick-up truck, slowly making my way and reminiscing of all the wonderful moments we had together. It was almost dusk as I approached that peaceful place. Though what I discovered there would be restful, it would not be a place of solace nor quiet.

Walking away from the truck and toward the site of my reclusion was silent enough, and the snow falling ever so slowly eased my mind and my soul. A small hill covered in wild blackberry bushes and a few trees that had not yet lost all their leaves hid my view as I approached my destination. Suddenly, my thoughts were disrupted when, out of nowhere, a man stopped me as I crested the hill. I had seen him earlier, he was one of the knights, and was acting as a sentinel to halt my progress. Although temporarily stopped, I could see past him, and noticed that there was a large campfire burning and a company of gentlemen standing and kneeling around it. The sentinel called out to the others, "*He has arrived,*" and when he said this, all heads turned my way.

My uncle, now one of the Twelve, came to me and greeted me with a most curious salutation. "*We have been waiting for you,*" were his exact words. How did he know anything about my plans? I told no one, other than my grandmother, where I would be, and she was not prone to release any information given her in confidence. He proceeded to usher me toward the others, and though perplexed, I honestly was delighted with such fine companionship on this cold night.

The fire was raging. There were twelve men gathered round it and four others acting as sentries in each direction. Just south of the fire was a big rock, and I had convalesced there on many occasions with my grandfather, especially as he got older. It was his favorite place to impart stories, yet at the time, it was my belief that they were just the fantastical ramblings of an old man. I always adored the tales and thought as to how marvelous such fables were shared between grandfathers and grandsons.

It was here, too, that he would teach me sayings and ways to say certain things I was meant to memorize all of them, as if they were to be recalled in some future dispensation. Today, for the first time, I understood my recollection of the rituals and the events that had transpired. They were all parts of the stories he had gifted me.

One by one, each of the Twelve introduced themselves. They told me of how they had met my grandfather, not one introduction was the same. Each had something special they held dear about him. One, who was now a governor, talked about the prayers offered up for his wife in a great time of need, and the solemness of a very windy and cold funeral to honor another fallen warrior. Another, now the Attorney General of the Republic of Tennessee, recalled a hallowed graveyard visit to show respect for a true son of our cause, and the hardships of many attacks in the early days. There were men of high office, but there were also men of what my grandfather would call "great necessity." There was one they all fondly called the "Tyrant," who had compelled the men to move ever forward.

Each of the Twelve had suffered, been discouraged, fought from time to time amongst themselves, but all remembered they had been called to a greater purpose. As the night went on, old wounds were healed, all suspicions were laid to rest, and friendships that had waned over the years were made fresh again. Mortality has a way of reminding us of that which is important, and in their memories, they all knew my grandfather was one to try and mend broken fences among brothers, especially over a few sips of Tennessee whiskey.

There was plenty of whiskey to go around. As the night grew longer and air got colder, the heat from the fire and abundant libations warmed our company. Then, my uncle asked me if I could recall the story of the "Keeper of the Fire"? I nodded in affirmation, all the men grew silent and respectful, and I was asked to tell the tale as it had been given to me.

The mood had changed. There was a seriousness in the cold night air. I focused on being exact in my recollection. What I had taken as mythology, these men thought to be something much different. There was gravity to the story in the hearts of these men, from the ghost like figure at the fire, the sword, grey coat, cavalier hat, and, of course, the man to which the flame had been passed. Each, to a man, affirmed the validity of the story, as it had been passed down. Each of the Twelve had received the story in succession from the one whom had experienced the event on a night just like tonight, yet many years ago. That man was my grandfather, and now it was to be passed down again.

All the knights arose, and the sentries turned inward, staring directly at me. They did not move for some time and were silent for what seemed an eternity. Then the Twelve moved to encircle me. I had not noticed that all of them were dressed in grey cloaks, and each was outfitted with a lapel pin distinguishing their order and their clans.

The oldest knight called to the others, *"There must always be 12 knights per clan and there must always be 12 clans to complete in the Brotherhood."*

The knights asked in unison, *"Who is worthy?"*

Without hesitation and driven by pure instinct, I yelled out, *"None! I will keep the fire!"*

At that, one knight placed a grey coat on my shoulders, a cavalier hat in my hands, and I knelt before all the knights. The oldest knight whispered a secret name into my ear, only known by the other knights. My head bowed, he took the sword that had been passed down through the generations and affirmed me as one of the knights, completing once again the hundred and forty-four.

They all stayed and welcomed me into the brotherhood but as the night lingered, they all dispersed, leaving my uncle and myself. Finally, we had time to remember a man as just a father and grandfather. We laughed and wept in his honor. It was some time after midnight when my uncle gave me a few instructions to possess my attention till the morning, then he departed. I spent the next hours in vigil to prepare my soul for the task ahead of me. Eventually, I drifted off to sleep, covered in a heavy woolen blanket next to the fire that was still rather large.

As the sun began to break and the darkness relinquished its hold, a thick fog still resting on the campsite, I awoke suddenly. There was the sound of rustling around the fire, perhaps it was an animal coming close to warm itself, or my uncle returning to check on me, but it was not. A man suited in grey sat at the fire, added some wood bringing up the flame, tipped his hat to me, smiled as if he was pleased with the events of the night before, and walked away…

If you have read this story and want to be part of something bigger than yourself, be worthy of recruitment into the legend. Sacrifice for something greater than you. A tap on your shoulder to join the ranks of a treasured few may someday greet you into the history books of your people. Become mythological, Southern man.

Deo Vindice!

About the Author: Father O'Dabney is the pen name of a longtime writer for Identity Dixie, focusing on poetry, fiction, and cultural issues related to reviving a Christ focused Southern identity.

Born on a reservation in the Carolinas, O'Dabney spent his childhood growing-up in the sand, salt, and sea of the Low Country of South Carolina and maturing into adulthood in the unreconstructed sanctuary of North Florida. Theologically educated, with deep blue-collar roots, Father O' Dabney is an evangel of Southern Nationalism. Married for 40 years, with seven children, and a joyous onslaught of grandchildren, O' Dabney is refocusing his vision toward agrarianism, fraternal brotherhoods, and helping to build communities that will be anti-fragile in the coming collapse of the decaying American empire.

The Committed Southern Remnant, *By Jude Ruffin*

The South and her people have been defeated by war, subjugated by the Empire, and now undergo cultural genocide as every last vestige of our culture is co-opted, erased, besmirched, or destroyed. Our people are subjected to every form of degradation, from the mocking of our speech to the lampooning of our national character. The Southerner is the Emmanuel Goldstein in this age of neoliberal madness. Yet, despite everything, we still exist. We have not been annihilated, much to the chagrin of the opponents of Dixie.

See, Dixie can never die as long as one of her native sons still draws breath. The South still remains largely recalcitrant to the Empire's moral decay, even parts of Dixie ruled by those that hate her. Thankfully, her most loyal children remain Unreconstructed rebels to this day, a fact that enrages to no end the modern-day carpetbagger, the acolyte of progressivism, and the Yankee. The

Southern tongue can still be heard throughout Dixie, despite modern America's rabid hatred for such a genuine, authentic, and refined speech. The universal symbol of resistance to liberal and globalist tyranny, the Confederate Battle Flag, is still flown from Maryland to Texas. We endure, even in the Empire's decline.

People come and go throughout the South. The interstate system allows easy travel and access to our lands. The American gypsy is not loyal to his soil, or even his blood for that matter. He travels, and eventually squats over a piece of ground, for money, food, the weather, and leisure. These motivations are not tied to anything substantial, there's no fidelity in that way of thinking. Unlike the Yankee nomad, we are guided by a timeless allegiance to the soil. It is ours and forever will be, our ancestors paid that price for us. This will remain a mystery to the non-Southerner because he cannot fathom such devotion, since he has none himself.

It is not just the ground under our feet, either. It is the blood in the dirt, the sweat in the red clay, and tears in the sand. Our fathers, uncles, brothers, mothers, sisters, cousins, grandparents, great grandparents, and those further in the forgotten past, they all rest in our Southern soil. It is ours and we do not forget the dead, lest we shame their memory and our honor. We, the Remnant of the Southland, carry on their legacy and their memory. As the wheel of progress turns, so will the animus and hatred for our people, including our venerated dead, those with us today, and our posterity. We have no choice but continue to persevere.

As Dixie's Remnant, it is our duty to press ever forward, to deny the zeitgeist that desires to subdue us, and thrive among the ruins of something that was beautiful. We are charged with retaking everything. If given the choice, many of us would rather have been born in another age, one no doubt with other challenges, but not the existential crisis facing us today. However, here we are, we have nothing except for our duty to our people and our individual honor. That will always be enough for men with stout hearts staring down tremendous odds.

Every Southern monument that is torn down strengthens our resolve. Every road or city street that is renamed toughens us. Every defaced headstone and defiled grave are stark reminders of the dark malice set upon our people. We do not forget, and we do not forgive - to do so would be to surrender to a people that salivate at the thought of iconoclasm and our demographic ruination. We will never be let alone, as our rivals have one endgame – the utter elimination of the last bastion of traditionalism on the North American continent.

We will be called villains by strangers, evil by fair-weather friends, and, God forbid, traitors by some of our family. Why? Because we are free men and women. We would rather be free and poor, than servile and wealthy. We are Southerners, the most despised people within the American Empire. We are Unreconstructed, with a legitimate heritage and culture that is unique and worthy of defending. We are the Remnant of the long-dead Republic and its heir, Dixie, and, as such, we will be reviled by those that embrace such insane modern doctrines such as state-supported infanticide and egalitarianism.

Our world will, unfortunately, get much worse. Within a decade, practically all monuments to our Southern ancestors will be destroyed. Even those hidden away in the backwater corners of Dixie will not be spared. The Left will find them, and its legions will destroy them. They have an insatiable appetite for iconoclasm, and government provided immunity. After the South is hallowed out of her monuments, they will march on the Founders and anyone and everything else found not acceptable in the ever-evolving progressive grievance culture.

The cultural deterioration will worsen over time. Transgenderism will become increasingly enforceable by the American Empire, either de factor or de jure, and in various invasive and offensive capacities that only our nightmares can entertain. It will be far worse than what we view from a distance on the internet. Rather, it'll be at your front door. All television, film, and music will be fundamentally more unpleasant than it is even now (as difficult as that is to imagine). The straight, White, male antagonist will be culturally codified as the standard villain in practically all storytelling. The prevailing narrative will be socially structured that you are "hateful," even more so than now. To speak out will risk even greater social ostracism and, possibly, legal repercussions.

The future will be a perfect environment for succumbing to mental and spiritual paralysis. Taking a steady regimen of demoralization freezes you, it shuts you down. A man becomes a defeatist when all he sees around him is defeat and despair. He can do nothing but contemplate and wallow in defeat. This cultural submission is the path of the beaten down, emotional coward. We must ensure that our Remnant does not submit to mental subjugation. The Left desires our trepidation and eventual surrender.

Rather than cave and destroy ourselves to the American Empire, we must become the

Southern Remnant within their world. But, instead of serving our masters of the managed decline, we *outwardly* serve no one. We sit silently and say nothing with regard to the decaying state, as Nicolás Gómez Dávila once wrote, "When nothing in society deserves respect, we should fashion for ourselves in solitude new silent loyalties." And, in that solitude and watching from our grim eyes, we *inwardly* focus on the Southern people and the path forward. No smiles or grimaces as the situation deteriorates, just a silent understanding that no one will save our people, except us, the Southern Remnant.

Moving forward, you must sacrifice for your people. Enough with the infighting and enough with the wastefulness of internet culture. Enough with the asinine personalities that fizzle out within a year. Enough with the race to the "hottest take." Enough with the negativity and blind hate. We will never win on hate alone. Hate is not enough to save our people; you must love your people. No one sacrifices for hate - they sacrifice for love.

How do you sacrifice? Simple, you sacrifice your time and resources for your people. You raise awareness of our plight through content creation. It takes minimal effort to write your thoughts down and provide them to a Southern Nationalist outlet. Only our message can combat the narrative. If our message reaches one Southerner, and it resonates with them, then we have awakened one more person to our cause. If you cannot create content, then at least share the content across social media. If you cannot share the content, financially support the content creators. You must do something.

There are other ways to sacrifice. Help a needy family. Raise funds for a fellow traveler down on his luck or support his widow. The South has never been immune to natural disasters, help our people when these unfortunate events happen. Review your brother's resume and give him pointers to advance his career. Again, these have never been accomplished with hate in our hearts but love for our people.

Sacrifice requires action. You must force yourself *to do*. You cannot sit back and passively allow the passing of our world and our people. It requires a mental, physical, and even spiritual commitment to act – to write, to network, to build, to protect, to congratulate, to undermine, to beguile, to astonish, to outlast, to do and succeed. This is required of the Southern Remnant.

Long after this Dark Age has come and gone, we will still be here. Those that hate Christ, sanity, civilization, the South, hierarchy, and tradition will be forgotten in the dust. Their memory will be consigned to oblivion. However, we will still be here because we represent the natural order, an eternal state of things. We are in service to our Lord, our land, and our people. This elemental commitment makes for an immortal cause, something that modernity, no matter what, can never extinguish.

Who are you in your heart? Who do you love? What do you love?

I am a Nationalist. I believe in the fundamental right of all distinct peoples to determine their own future without molestation. I love my people. I love my South. I love my wife, children, my grandchildren, and my great-grandchildren within whom Southern blood pumps through their hearts, born and grown on Southern soil. To this, I am committed. Are you committed? Do you know the meaning of commitment?

Commitment is a total emotional, physical, and mental state of determination toward a goal. The man without commitment is not a man. He is a cog in a wheel, devoid of purpose. He is nothing.

Commitment is the young boy on Parris Island running another step further through his painful exhaustion to earn the title of "Marine." Commitment is marching through snow without shoes to fight a superior British Army, because you hope to create a country of your own. Commitment is charging the Yankee lines one more time through unrelenting fire because they have invaded your homeland. Commitment is jumping off a landing ship at Okinawa, because your family back home is imperiled by an enemy who has proven he will strike them down if you do not kill them there.

Commitment is waking up early to read your Bible because God's Word means Salvation to you. Commitment is working long hard hours because you want your wife and children to be fed. Commitment is scraping, saving, fighting, and beating the odds so that you can build an enduring business that will ultimately lay a pathway for the future of your family and your people.

Commitment is spending every waking moment knowing failure is not an option.

Commitment is making one more deadlift because you know your bodies must be hardened for the future that awaits. Commitment is one more squat because you may have to carry your spouse on your back as the enemy comes to kill her. Commitment is making yourself faster because your body must be prepared for the privation your enemies will impose upon you.

Commitment is continuing to work toward the betterment and independence of your people even though you have lost your job, your livelihood, and your associates. Commitment is continuing to fight against the overwhelming odds that surround your cause because your people mean more to you than the pain you will surely endure. Commitment is standing in the face of your enemies and letting them know you will not bow down no matter what they do – and after they strike – telling them again.

Commitment is hard. Commitment is not comfortable. It would have been easier for me to accept the modern narrative and live the easy life of a well-educated, white-collar professional. It would have been easier to put blinders on to the murder and rape of my people by savages – cheered on by their elite masters. It would have been easier for me to ignore the kneeling protests and enjoyed football games, while I got fatter on my couch. But I chose the harder path. I became committed to something more than me. I became committed to my people.

I am committed to my Holy Triune God. I am committed to my family. I am committed to my Southern nation.

Failure is not an option for our people. The world within which we suddenly find ourselves seeks the eradication of all that is good. It seeks the death of my people – a people whom I love. Commitment is the manifestation of a love greater than yourself. This is something that our adversaries do not understand.

Marxists of all stripes – from neoconservative Republicans to Maoists – cannot endure the continuation of distinct Nations. Tribalism is anathema to the compelled collective. This is why groups like Black Lives Matter hate the nuclear family. This is why neoconservative Republicans push globalized capitalism over national interest. Distinct peoples make collectivism impossible.

The irony of the so-called Marxist-inspired "Resistance" is that it enjoys the full support of the

U.S. Government, monied elites, and big corporations. They are not resisting anything. Antifa is the Establishment.

The problem for the higher elites in Western society is that they firmly believe they can control the beast they unleashed. The original goal was to ensure no manifestation of national identity coalesced into a successful movement. White Nationalist content producers are allowed to thrive because elites know they will never succeed. Southern Nationalism, on the other hand, has the potential to erode confidence in the status quo among a core component of global capitalism: potential military recruits. If Southern Nationalist messages resonate among young Southerners, the potential for their volunteer military service diminishes. This is likely the reason that the military has taken a sudden anti-Southern turn and has sped up its goals to recruit more minorities. Something is changing in Southern boys as evidenced in the missed recruitment goals of the Department of Defense in the once dependable

South. They will need black boys to die overseas moving forward and the government adjusted its strategy to get them.

Going back to Marxists, the problem for elites is that they do not understand that Marxists actually believe their own rhetoric. The notion that they will survive a future purge after dissidents are dispatched is laughable. Such elites never do. The Communist Party apparatchik in China and their businessmen allies form the entirety of China's multi-millionaires. They were not born to multigenerational elite families. They are descendants of Mao's henchmen and now serve as Xi's guard.

Southern Nationalists, such as the authors of this book, are not paid richly sums for our hard work; they are believers in the cause. They are committed. Southern Nationalists have suffered tremendous personal discomfort and loss, yet they have not relented. In fact, if anything, every dox has come with a renewed commitment to keep going. Balkanization talk is growing throughout the United

States and the seeds of that balkanization were ideologically sown by the Fire Eaters of the mid-19th Century. The roots of their words are now blooming thanks to an expansion of the Overton Window we have helped facilitate through targeting the Southern zeitgeist. We are the Southern Remnant that stands unconquered and Unreconstructed.

With every Confederate monument they tear down, a thousand new Southern Nationalists are born. With every company they target for non-conformity, a thousand new Southern Nationalists are born. With every young Southern boy whom they mock for his patriotism, as he returns to his native soil in a body bag from a foreign war, a thousand new Southern Nationalists are born.

And I will do my part to make thousands more.

About the Author: Jude Ruffin (pseudonym) is a devout Christian and hails from a secluded and still-Southern farm country in the Delmarva region. Mr. Ruffin comes from a long, distinguished line of Virginians. Like many throughout his lineage, Mr. Ruffin attended the College of William & Mary and the same graduate school as Padraig Martin. Prior to entering semi-retirement, Jude taught at a university in the Middle East in the late-1970s and throughout the1980s. After leaving the university, Mr. Ruffin worked in several former Soviet Republics on government reform throughout the 1990s and early-2000s. He has four grown children, eighteen grandchildren, and two great-grandchildren.

Liberal Democracy vs. Organic Nationalism: A Template for the South, *By Dr. Michael Hill*

Since the 18th Century Enlightenment, the West has made an idol of Liberal Democracy. It has in effect become the political default position of most Westerners, including most Americans. We accept it as "right" without critical examination. In fact, I don't think it incorrect to say that Liberal Democracy has become the civic religion of America and the West.

In American politics, voting majorities marshaled every two or four years have become our gods. They dictate to us how we shall live and die. Most say they wouldn't have it any other way. That would be un-American. To be patriotic citizens, we must live with the results of the ballot, be it in a general election, a Supreme Court ruling, or a Congressional vote. The verdict is sacrosanct because it was reached through the democratic process of majority vote. We can grouse and complain about it, but we see ourselves bound by it.

Otherwise, how could we claim to be "good Americans?"

But our classroom civics books did not tell us that majority rule only works where there is already a consensus of sorts on the fundamental issues within a particular society. For instance, in a Christian country that enjoys a high degree of homogeneity in its racial and ethnic make-up, language, institutions, and inherited culture, most matters up for a vote are largely superficial policy issues. They don't tamper with the agreed-upon foundations of the society. However, in a multicultural and multiracial polyglot empire, such as ours is today, the concept of majority rule is often fraught with dire (and even deadly) consequences for the losers, especially if the winners bear a grudge. As multiculturalism destroys civic identity, racial and ethnic identity rises to take its place. This is obviously not conducive to civic peace and prosperity.

As I write at the start of 2023, there are projections that these United States – and our beloved Southland – will have a White minority by 2040 (or before, depending on immigration policy and minority birth rates). Simply put, that will mean the end of society as we know it. You and Joe Biden may be okay with this, but I'm not.

Who stands to lose by this devil's bargain? The descendants of America's founding stock will be the losers. As a native White Southerner, I'm primarily concerned about the future of the South. Our ancestors bequeathed us a society based on Christian moral principles, the English language, racial (and some degree of ethnic) homogeneity, and British legal and political institutions. All this will be gone with the wind if we don't stand against the unholy leftist trinity of "tolerance, diversity, and multiculturalism."

Perhaps Americans in other regions outside the South are quite happy with the idea of giving their region of the country away to minorities and their White leftist enablers. But if the rest of the country is determined to go straight to hell, is the

South obliged to go along for the ride just so "democracy" can be upheld? I state that it is not.

It is time that Southerners - the descendants of European, Christian peoples who settled the Southern regions of North America - make a fundamental decision whether to break with the Enlightenment idea of Liberal Democracy and to embrace the concept of Southern nationhood. Southern nationhood is nothing less than the acknowledgment that Southerners' survival (see above definition), well-being, and independence should be the primary considerations for the here-and-now as well as for the future. If current political arrangements do not promote our survival, well-being, and independence, then they should be cast aside for new arrangements that do promote these ends. This includes democracy in all its forms.

What the South must embrace for its survival is Organic Nationalism. What is that you ask? It is a form of nationalism in which the political state (the government) receives its legitimacy from the organic unity of those whom it serves. In other words, it is a true nation-state such as historic France, Germany, or England. Hallmarks of that organic unity are race/ethnicity, language, culture and folk customs, and religion. It is therefore a "nation"—a distinct people or Folk—in the most primal and fundamental sense. By its very nature it is conservative in that its main function is to conserve a society that will defend the lives, liberty, and property of the people who comprise it. Their survival, well-being, and independence are paramount. Conversely, they reject the top-down universal hegemony of the elites.

What would a South that embraced Organic Nationalism look like? It would be a South that returned to its European roots but with plenty of leeway given for those cultural attributes that are uniquely Southern. It would embrace and celebrate as good and wholesome all its peculiarities without apology and without embarrassment - its literature, language and dialect, religious faith, folkways, songs, and overall worldview. It would also draw from that deep cultural well that is Europe, taking the best of that and calling it our own as well.

That the organic South is both European and extra-European offers us no conundrum. After all, we have been in Dixie for four hundred years, and that experience has turned various European ethnicities into a loose but cohesive unity known as "Southern." Thus, we have one foot in Europe and the other in Dixie, and that makes us a distinct people, a real nation unlike any other in the world.

Out of this organic diversity - this rather deep and wide DNA gene pool - has come a true nation - the South. Yes, there are others among us, some in sizable and growing numbers (blacks and mestizos, respectively), but they are not "us" and this is not their nation of which I speak. As to the former, we will have to work out some arrangement based on goodwill from both sides. As to the latter, they do not belong here and must be deported, and the borders sealed against them. As for others, we would be wise to take things on a case-by-case basis.

Unlike the South, the United States is not a "nation;" rather, it is a failed leftist experiment. I do not believe our Founders intended it to be such, but nonetheless it has become that. As such, it should have no appeal to true Southerners. Indeed, it should have no moral purchase on our loyalty.

The American Empire has bound its identity to the Enlightenment idea of Liberal Democracy and all that it entails. Moreover, it has compounded the problem by willingly and wittingly committing itself to becoming a multicultural, polyglot empire in which democratic institutions are manipulated by the ruling elite for the benefit of favored groups.

As I look at my precious children and grandchildren, I shudder to think what will happen to them and their descendants when they become the numerical political and actual demographic minority. Revenge – "getting even" – will be a commonplace occurrence as our folk are attacked and robbed of life, liberty, and property with impunity in the name of social justice or some other fabricated right of man. Will the rights of our children and grandchildren be protected by the new regnant majority who are not products of Western Christian civilization? Or will a majority of wolves vote to devour a minority of sheep? I think you know the answer.

Southern Nationalists, unlike Americans under the globalists' sway, are wedded not to a universal proposition: equality, democracy, or the rights of man, but to a real historical order based on place and kin. That entity is the Real South, not that wretched thing called the New South. If we Southern Whites are to survive as a distinct people with a physical place to live, work, and worship, then we must never waver from this commitment.

We Southerners must embrace a new paradigm. We must get "out of the box" in which our enemies have placed us. We must have a new organizing principal, by means of a new template: Organic Nationalism. It is the answer for the South if we are serious about the survival, well-being, and independence of the Southern people. That means the rejection of the status quo of living in a multicultural empire that sucks our lifeblood.

The late M. E. Bradford in his *Remembering Who We Are: Observations of a Southern Conservative* (University of Georgia Press, 1985) deals at length, as the title suggests, with cultural identity and historical memory. He cites the following lines by the protagonist of Stark Young's *So Red the Rose*, Hugh McGehee, as he sends his son off to join the Confederate Army: "It's not to our credit to think we began today and it's not to our glory to think we end today. All through time we keep coming into the shore like waves, like waves. You stick to your blood, son; there's a fierceness in blood can bind you up with a long community of life." The most eloquent of anti-Federalists, Patrick Henry, chided those who thought that "All things should be made new" by reminding them that "we are descended from a people whose government was founded on liberty; our glorious grandfathers of Great Britain made liberty the foundation of everything... We draw that spirit of liberty from our British ancestors." Bradford, Young, and Henry all caution us that it is from our fathers, and not from universal (or even particular) abstractions, that we draw our sustenance as a separate, distinct, God-ordained people.

Yet, for the past half-century, liberals and neoconservatives alike have been seeking to discredit the idea that a man's first temporal allegiance is to kith and kin. It is the self-appointed task of social engineers to reshape Creation according to their own ideas of good and evil. They are, as it were, attempting to rebuild the Tower of Babel and, in the bargain, are seeking to nullify the Biblical and historical reality of true nationhood. The cult of equality (both of individuals and cultures), according to Bradford, is the new "opiate of the masses." Totalitarians of all stripes today champion equality by pushing for an "open door" immigration policy that favors the Third World. They care not whether the massive influx of Muslims, Latinos, and other non-Western peoples poses a threat to the racial, ethnic, and cultural balance of our country. Rather, since the Left holds sacred the "rights of man," they view America as the world's first universal nation, dedicated to the proposition that all men and cultures are created equal.

If the idea that America is indeed a mere proposition nation is to be realized, then the narrowly defined "posterity" of our forefathers must be broadened to include the whole of Emma Lazarus's "wretched refuse." The Immigration and Naturalization Act of 1965 and subsequent legislation and judicial edicts have turned America's immigration policy inside out by allowing for the influx of millions upon millions of non-Europeans while largely closing the "Golden Door" to European immigrants. Both Third World legals and illegals are encouraged to maintain their own cultures and languages while partaking of the largesse available to them at the expense of taxpaying citizens.

If Southerners do not control the South's destiny but are swamped by an alien people carrying an alien ideology, then even under the best of circumstances this situation will eventually weaken and destroy our civilization. Simply put, this "other" will lack the desire, understanding, and intellectual capacity to preserve our vital institutions. More importantly, it will physically displace the descendants of the founding stock and we will cease to control the homeland bequeathed us by generations of noble and honorable men and women - our ancestors. We will suffer a fate perhaps worse than that of Rome itself. Already, radical Latinos have launched a Reconquista of our southern borders while radical Muslims build mosques and talk openly of jihad in our midst. Simultaneously, federal judges are thwarting the efforts of Americans of Western European ancestry to turn back the tide rising against us. It is abundantly clear with whom the Establishment elites side on this crucial issue.

If we Southerners are to survive and prosper on the lands given us by our forebears, then we would do well to adopt the attitude of historian Frank L. Owsley (one of the Twelve Southerners who contributed to *I'll Take My Stand*). Owsley, in his seminal work *Plain Folk of the Old South* (LSU Press, 1949), writes: "The term 'folk' has for its primary meaning a group of kindred people, forming a tribe or nation [in the truest sense of the word]; a people bound together by ties of race, language, religion, custom, tradition, and history… A folk thus possesses a sense of solidarity and is quite different from a conglomerate mass of people. It has most if not all of the characteristics of nationalism [again, properly defined]. Indeed, it may be contended with much force that there can be no true nationalism where the population does not constitute a folk." Owsley contends that the "Southern people, according to these several characteristics, were a genuine folk long before the Civil War [*sic*]." Moreover, he tells us that the "greatest single factor, perhaps, in developing the

Southern population into a genuine American folk was the common national origin of the bulk of the people… [T]he Southern people prior to 1860 were predominantly British… Appearance, the indefinable qualities of personality, and their manners and customs, particularly their distinctive speech, set them apart from the inhabitants of the other sections of the United States, and in this way strengthened their sense of kinship."

Southern Nationalism of the organic variety should have as its primary objective the preservation of our people – kith and kin – on their ancestral lands. Independence will do the South little good if we fail to preserve ourselves as a distinct people group inhabiting a certain piece of Creation. Once we secure our future as "the Southern people," then, and only then, can we go about the business of gaining our independence. Therefore, we support a return to a society and civilization based on allegiance to kith and kin rather than to an impersonal state wedded to multiculturalism, diversity, tolerance, the rights of man, and other similar leftist abstractions.

The leaders and the rank-and-file of our various Southern Nationalist organizations must be hardliners who insist that quite apart from political ideals, we take our stand *in* the historic South and *for* the people – White Southerners – who made the historic South what it is. The South is not a universal idea any more than Scotland, France, or Serbia. Instead, the South was and is a true *nation* built on the realities of place and kinship that we must revitalize if we are to survive and prosper.

At its core, the South is British-Western European and Christian. Should this change, then the South as we know it shall be no more. As the late Russell Kirk wrote in *America's British Culture*: "If somehow the British elements could be eliminated from all the cultural patterns of the United States, Americans would be left with no coherent culture in public or in private life." He continues with a salient warning: "We Americans live… in an era when the general outlines and institutions of our inherited culture still are recognizable; yet it does not follow that our children or our grandchildren, in the twenty-first century, will retain a great part of that old culture... The defence of inherited culture [and, I might add, the people who create and sustain that culture] must be conducted here and now, with what weapons may be snatched from the walls here on the darkling plain at the end of the twentieth century."

When we do endeavor to defend our own people and culture, liberals, neoconservatives, and politically correct "Rainbow Confederates" hurl at us the usual invectives: "racists," "xenophobes," and "reactionaries." It is past time that we turn a deaf ear to these bogus charges and set about resisting any attempts to reconstruct a modern Tower of Babel on the rubble of our Southern civilization. Victory goes to the bold.

We Southern Nationalists should want to see a South where our borders are sealed against massive immigration. We should seek a South where the interests of the Southern people are protected from the ravages of multiculturalism and so-called diversity. We need a South whereby a prosperous, self-confident, and distinct people – our people – can welcome into its ranks by its own choice and on its own terms productive and sympathetic immigrants. We must create a South that will be a beacon to those nations that wish to defend a traditional way of life against the purveyors of abstract ideologies and a new world order. This begins by creating a South where Southerners shall know beyond a doubt that the fundamental question to be answered, as M. E. Bradford insists, is not the Federalists' "What shall we do?" but Patrick Henry's "Who are we?" Indeed, when we know who we are and are willing to defend ourselves and our posterity, then we shall be a truly free people with a bright future. If we fail to grasp the gravity of this basic question, we shall end up in the proverbial "dustbin of history," and deservedly so.

In order for Southerners to survive and prosper, I contend that we must simply re-define along the lines of Organic Nationalism the political and social entity to which we belong - the Southern nation. In that polity, our interests and moral principles will hold sway, and we can determine who gets to be called "citizen" and who exercises the right to vote and participate in other civic matters. No more being ruled by alien, universalist elites. No more kowtowing to the interests of Massachusetts, New York, and California. The Southern nation will be run by Southerners in the interest of Southerners. Will that not be a glorious and blessed day?

About the Author: Dr. J. Michael Hill was born in 1951 in Marion Co., Alabama. He attained his Ph.D. in history from The University of Alabama in 1985. Dr. Hill is the author or editor of three books: <u>Celtic Warfare</u>, <u>Fire and Sword</u>, and <u>The Grey Book (ed.)</u>. Dr. Hill taught history at The University of Alabama from 1978-1996 and at Stillman College from 1985-1999. He is the Founder and President of The League of the South, 1994-present. He is a proud Charlottesville veteran, among many other interesting adventures.

Reconsidering Our Nation, *By Anne Wilson Smith*

Most Americans think of their nation as fifty states, with familiar outlines on a map. They think of the Founding Fathers, the red, white and blue flag, and the Capitol building at Washington, DC. Most modern Americans have also, to some degree or another, internalized the "melting pot" philosophy of civic nationalism and believe that shared ideas, such as those written in the Declaration of Independence, provide the bonds that unite American citizens. However foreign the notion may seem to us now, traditionally nations have been understood to be groups of specific people connected by shared tangible connections like history, culture, and race, rather than by nebulous ideas like "equality" and "freedom."

The United States of America has, through mass immigration, political subversion, and aggressive propaganda campaigns, been expanded, twisted, and distorted into something unrecognizable to those of us old enough to remember the Reagan era and before. Furthermore, it is evident to any honest observer that the American Empire - with its weak and corrupt political class, a populace crippled by cultural and racial conflict, the normalization of ineptitude and immorality, and the loss of respect on the world stage - is in its death throes. Americans can no longer define ourselves by our enfeebled founding documents or the crumbling structures of our once-great institutions. It is time for all Americans, and specifically Southerners, to re-evaluate what we think of as our "nation."

As electoral campaigns endeavor to turn "red" states "blue," with pressure from Wall Street, Hollywood, and Washington DC, Southern states have been flooded with money and immigrants (from both foreign nations and other American states). They promote an agenda that is hostile to that of the historic Southern population. We must ask: in what way are the state borders meaningful today, if at all? If proponents of the "blue" and "red" ideologies are forced into proximity to further the goals of our elite chess masters, do these groups of people automatically become compatriots in any meaningful sense? Of course not. Our political borders are increasingly irrelevant, and our elected lawmakers increasingly non-representative. It is time to alter the paradigm.

The American concept of "nation" must shift away from one that is defined by historical political structures and geographical borders, to one that is defined by the extended families of historically related peoples who share similar lifestyles and values. As ideological and racial clashes continue to increase across the United States, pressure will mount for people to align into these more natural and meaningful factions. In effect, secession will naturally manifest.

As the empire formerly known as these United States continues to disintegrate, the Southern people are at an advantage with regards to our sense of identity. Many White Americans who advocate for nationalism flounder when searching for a sense of identity. Some look to ancient European religions for connection with their roots, while others seek unity based upon common characteristics among White people of diverse backgrounds. These inorganic and loosely defined qualities are a weak basis upon which to build a future. Southerners face many challenges, but we are not burdened with this particular struggle. For better or worse (depending on whom you ask) Southerners have always been considered a distinct subset of the American population. Whatever problems we may have, one thing is certain: we are a real people.

What is distinctive about the South? The most obvious characteristics are those of speech, manner, dress, music, pastimes, and cuisine, and most Southerners easily recognize and readily embrace these things. Such regional traits are non-threatening to the powerful, and may even be considered quaint and charming, and so have not been aggressively targeted for eradication. Other qualities are less apparent but perhaps more important – differences in values and character. These characteristics include clannishness, adherence to traditional gender norms, a spirit of self-reliance, and skepticism towards authority. Our sense of identity has been diluted by immigration and warped by generations of hostile propaganda and education. Still, we remain a recognizable and self-aware subset of Americans. There is much upon which to build a way forward.

One critical, defining characteristic of the Southerner is that of a lived Christian faith, with a concomitant worldview that maintains belief in the fallen nature of humanity, the reality of evil, the inevitability of suffering, and the eventual accountability of each person to our Maker for our wrongs. A Christian worldview also imbues one with a sense of humility, and a certainty that the world cannot be perfected through the designs of men whose knowledge is limited and whose hearts are impure. This view manifests in a resistance to intrusive government and utopian leftist programs for "change," which is problematic for agents of the globalist agenda. Therefore, our history, heroes, and values have been targeted. Though damage has been done and she is less robust than she once was, we may have faith that the heart of Dixie will continue to beat long after the corpse of Lincoln's empire has rotted away.

I believe there are many actions that peaceful people of good will can take to build a robust future for the millions of Southern people who abide in the remnants of these United States. How can we preserve what remains of our cherished culture, and build up a new way forward for the Southern people?

One simple but powerful step is to completely disengage from corporate entertainment. It is hard to overstate the damage done at the individual and societal level by the entertainment industry. We are coarsened, dulled, and severed from our roots and our Creator. Mass-produced entertainment is not only low quality, but it is often barely disguised, subversive propaganda produced by people, within and without the country, whom have a vested interest in undermining healthy cultural norms in general and Christian values in particular. Much of this "entertainment" singles out the South for derision or slander, which poisons the young against their own people and history.

Television viewing can be a comfortable habit, but consider the fact that we spend hundreds of dollars a month for the privilege of allowing people who hate us to pump toxic sludge into our living rooms. Cutting the cord not only saves money but takes away the crutch of spending time in a semi-vegetative state on the sofa, focused on superficial and sordid content created by the enemies of God. Make a conscious decision to turn your attention to activities that better nurture your family's heart and mind. As we disengage from the filthy pablum of foreign origin, and look inside to our creative Southern souls, we will begin to replace it with locally produced, organic, and God-honoring art, music, and literature.

On the subject of entertainment, there are a few topics that require extra commentary. One is "country" music. The genre is wildly popular, as it is one of the few overtly Southern expressions of culture still allowed by the titans of the entertainment industry. However painful if may be to acknowledge, subversion set to banjo music and sung with a twang is still subversion. The most promoted and awarded country music stars promote the same "values" as do the pop singers - they disavow "hate," (read: traditional mores and pro-White sentiment), promote degeneracy, and, for the most part, toe the progressive party line with regards to issues like gun rights and the Confederate Battle Flag. We have been gobbling up the crumbs of affirmation that come from the animated corpse of the music of our people. Reject this. Make the effort to seek out and embrace soulful and authentic live, locally produced music, and reacquaint yourself with classics.

College and professional sports, especially football, are another popular pastime that fails to feed the Southern soul. We have sublimated our urges to root for "our" city, state, and region into a meaningless diversion that enriches our enemies and undermines our values. Instead of being a "fan" of a professional sport, play or coach sports for your local or church league. You will not only avoid feeding the "woke" beast, but you will become more fit, get to know your neighbors, and provide a positive influence to young people in your community.

Changing our entertainment choices is only one aspect of the plan. The key to the revitalization of the Southern soul is disengaging from the global and reconnecting to the local and personal. Focus on building and nurturing relationships, particularly with the senior members of your family if you are still blessed with their presence. Learn from your elders and teach your children. Seek fellowship with like-minded community members, with the goal of building trust and support networks. These efforts serve to rekindle tribal bonds, the absence of which have left many of us without a sense of place or belonging.

Build, preserve, and maintain what you value. Most of us need to relearn independent life skills that the modern world has caused to become obsolete, like growing and storing food and raising animals, and building and maintaining shelter. Share what you know and learn what you do not. Preserve your family history. Buy hard copies of literature and history books which the cultural police might wish to "revise" or blacklist as the revolution marches forward. We can all be flame keepers of our own little bits of knowledge, tradition, and culture. Such activities will make you more fulfilled in the present, and more prepared to face an uncertain future. By building up things that are real and personal, we will reconnect to our own nature. The revitalization of the innate Southern soul is sure to follow.

The American Empire to which we have been bound, celebrates the superficial, fanciful, material and ephemeral. Southerners crave authenticity, purpose, and connection with things that are natural and eternal. Our young people are in desperate need of guidance from those who will tell abiding truth, and offer hope, clarity, and wisdom. Sometimes it is necessary to speak boldly, but if you cannot do that, asking a thoughtful question or making a gentle observation is often enough to plant a seed of thought that will bloom at a later time.

Most importantly, we need to seek the guidance and blessings of the Lord if we hope to flourish in the future. I believe that we are a people that have been blessed by God. We have been given greater trials, but this has made us more wise, grounded, and unified. We were gifted with inspiration in the form of godly leaders like Robert E. Lee and "Stonewall" Jackson. We may yet gain the favor of God and be restored, if we plea to Heaven. "If my people, which are called by my name, shall humble themselves, and pray, and seek my face, and turn from their wicked ways; then will I hear from heaven, and will forgive their sin, and will heal their land." (2 Chronicles 7:14, KJV).

The fall of the Empire will inevitably create distress and daunting challenges, but we do not need to wallow in despair. It may be true that the institutions with which we grew up are dying or dead. Yet, we, the Southern people, are alive.

About the Author: Smith was born and raised in the Carolinas. She is an unassuming Southern belle by day, bold and opinionated writer by night. As the daughter of preeminent Southern historian and scholar Clyde N. Wilson, Smith was imbued from an early age with the understanding that Southern history and culture were widely slandered and misunderstood. It must be defended and cherished. Her life-long interest in religion, culture, and politics evolved over the years into a passion for writing that seeks to promote underappreciated truths, encourage the righteous, and affirm the value of the South and of Christianity.

Smith is the author of the most thorough and definitive record of the events that took place at Unite the Right in 2017, <u>Charlottesville Untold: Inside Unite the Right</u>. She also authored <u>Robert E. Lee: A History Book for Children</u>. Smith is the founder and managing editor of the website Reckonin. She lives in Columbia, SC with her husband and two children.

Americanism: Death of the South, *By Rick Dirtwater*

Culture is not an abstraction, it is a living, breathing entity comprised of a people. If a people are virtuous, pious, and industrious, the culture will be a reflection of its people. Conversely, if a people deteriorate into depravity, apathy, and slovenliness, it will be mirrored in the culture. Culture, like a people, has a life cycle – from birth and its ascension to its decline. Cultural rebirth is possible, but it requires a Herculean effort to stave off decline, particularly when internal and external pressures are advocating for its collapse, or when triggering the renascence of a culture long deceased.

To be clear, Southern culture will not survive as long as it is tied to the American Empire – both politically and socially. At present, Southern culture is a sub-category of the prevailing American "multiculturalism." However, it is a reviled culture (and people) within these United States, as both Southern culture and the traditional Southern people are diametrically opposed to modern Americanism. For Southern Nationalists, one of the primary concerns regarding Southern culture is that it will be absorbed and consumed by Americanism should the Southern states remain in a political union with the United States government. American culture is already exported throughout the globe, and its primary aim is to destroy all indigenous peoples and cultures within its path.

Domestically, the American Empire requires all cultures within its realm to be devoured by modern Americanism. In turn, this will produce a more docile, predictable, and, more importantly, controllable population. This aggressive cultural digestion applies even to Protestant-heavy Heritage America, traditional Catholics, and all the way down to recent Muslim immigrants. In the end, all groups inside the sphere of American influence will become "good little Americans." However, what is Americanism, or modern American culture?

The current American culture is not John Wayne and apple pie. It is certainly not gun-toting, country music blaring, Bible thumping reactionaries in pick-up trucks (those are elements of Southern culture, and typically exaggerated and extracted to rural, "country" areas of these United States). Old American culture had many positive things, but it now acts as an internal foil to contemporary Americanism. American culture is also not pro-family or pro-Christian, it is even vehemently opposed to good health, financial stability, literacy, and common sense. Americanism is a lewdness unfathomable to the Western world a century ago, a promotion of stupidity and imprudence warned about in Aesop's Fables, and holds a deep loathing for Christianity, masculinity, aesthetics, and its foundational history and people.

In short, Americanism can best be described as a 24/7 commercial starring crossdresser RuPaul as he twerks and pitches the benefits of a predatory reverse home mortgage to obese diabetics and simpletons. It is masquerading flashy bright colors and hypnotic jingles for mental peasants that have had their natural uncanny valley instincts programmed out of them through a subscription streaming service and public education. It wants its victims greatly in debt, medicated, mentally ill, stupid, sterile, and homogenized into a cocoa-colored McDonald's Happy Meal™.

Below are objective and measurable characteristics of Americanism. This is not information "made up" by a recalcitrant and angry Southern Nationalist. A cultural resurgence is not possible when you've reached this point of no return. American culture cannot be saved, much less reformed to 1950s Americana. Whereas there is still a glimmer of hope that Southern culture can be rescued through political balkanization and Southern sovereignty, Americanism is so atrocious and hated (internationally, and domestically via the Dissident Right) that it is unsustainable in the short to intermediate term – a culture that promotes child mutilation ("gender affirming care") over giving birth to real children has a short shelf-life, thank God.

***

Per Axios reporting in February of 2022[1], and based on a Gallup survey from 2021, the percentage of U.S. adults who identify as a homosexual or transexual has doubled over the past decade, from 3.5% in 2012 to 7% in 2021. "Generation Z" adults, who identify as such, increased from 10.5% in 2017 to 21% in 2021. Millennials, from ages 26 to 41, identifying as sexual reprobates also increased from 6% in 2012 to 10.5% in 2021. Note: this is based off data from a couple of years ago, and we're now in 2023. The likelihood that these concerning numbers will increase is certainly inevitable. A growing population of mentally ill perverts and homosexuals is not viable and, more alarmingly, we know how it spreads.

A Pew Research Center survey from 2021[2] observed that an increasing number of American

---

[1] Erin Doherty, Axios, "The number of LGBTQ-identifying adults is soaring," 19 February 2022, https://www.axios.com/2022/02/17/lgbtq-generation-z-gallup

[2] Anna Brown, Pew Research Center, "Growing share of childless adults in U.S. don't expect to ever have children," 19 November 2021, https://www.pewresearch.org/fact-tank/2021/11/19/growing-share-of-childless-adults-in-u-s-

adults, who are not already parents, are unlikely to ever have children, and their reasoning ranges from simply not wanting to have children to laughable concerns regarding "climate change." Some 44% of non-parents, from ages 18 to 49, indicated that it is unlikely or a certainty that they will never have children, an increase of 7% from the 37% who specified the same in a 2018 survey. In a 2022 study of 1,500 adults in Michigan[3], it was determined that 22% of them do not want to have children and, therefore, have opted to be "childfree." That same study estimates that childfree Americans are unfortunately quite common, comprising over one-fifth of the population (extrapolating the data throughout the domestic American Empire). Additionally, that 2022 analysis discovered that the "age-to-decision" (not having children) for most of these anti-natalist adults was "early in life." Wonder why? That's a rhetorical question.

---

dont-expect-to-ever-have-children/
[3] Jennifer Watling Neal and Zachary Neal, The Conversation, "Study: More than 1 in 5 US adults don't want children," 6 August 2022, https://www.newsnationnow.com/science/study-more-than-1-in-5-us-adults-dont-want-children

Americans are reading fewer books than at any point since 1990. According to Gallup[4], American adults read an average of 12.6 books in 2021. That's roughly three fewer books than what the same survey reported in 2016, and the smallest number Gallup has measured in more than three decades. The number of Americans reading more than 10 books per year dropped 8% between 2016 and 2021. Based on a 2021 Pew Research Center survey[5], nearly a quarter of American adults (23%) indicated that they did not read a book, in whole or even in part, in the previous year – in print, electronic, or even audio format. Furthermore, according to the U.S. Department of Education's own data[6], over half of Americans (54%) aged 16 to

---

[4] Jeffery M. Jones, Gallup, "Americans Reading Fewer Books Than in Past," 10 January 2022,
https://news.gallup.com/poll/388541/americans-reading-fewer-books-past.aspx

[5] Risa Gelles-Watnick and Andrew Perrin, Pew Research Center, "Who doesn't read books in America?," 21 September 2021, https://www.pewresearch.org/fact-tank/2021/09/21/who-doesnt-read-books-in-america/

[6] Jonathan Rothwell, Ph.D., Barbara Bush Foundation for Family Literacy, "Assessing the Economic Gains of Eradicating Illiteracy Nationally and Regionally in the United States," 8 September 2020, https://www.barbarabush.org/wp-

74 years old – or about 130 million people – read *below* the equivalent of a sixth-grade level. In case you need to be reminded, a sixth grader is usually 11 years old. At one point in Old America, Latin was routinely taught in grammar schools.

Per a OnePoll survey[7] of 2,000 American adults over the age of 30, six in ten (59%) Americans credited a celebrity with helping them through a challenging part of their lives. Those celebrities included Oprah Winfrey, Dwayne "The Rock" Johnson, Bear Grylls, Rebel Wilson, and Tyler Perry. They chose a celebrity over Christ, and this is not to be unexpected considering the status of Christianity within Americanism. In the early 1990s, about 90% of the people in the American Empire identified as Christian. In 2020, Christians accounted for about 64% of the United States population, including children[8]. That's a fairly

---

content/uploads/2020/09/BBFoundation_GainsFromEradicatingIlliteracy_9_8.pdf

[7] Entertainment Editors, <u>The New York Post</u>, "These celebs inspired people to push past their limits: poll," 4 October 2022, https://nypost.com/2022/10/04/these-celebs-inspired-people-to-push-past-their-limits-poll/

[8] Li Cohen, <u>CBS News</u>, "Christianity in the U.S. is quickly

significant decline and it occurred within the lifetime of all of the writers of this book. Additionally, those who are not affiliated with a religion has grown from 16% in 2007 to a staggering 30% in 2020[9]. Expect that number to rapidly increase year-over-year.

Current national trends indicate that each year more Americans die of overdoses—the majority of which involve opioid drugs - than died in the entirety of the Vietnam War, the Korean War, or any armed conflict since the end of World War II[10]. Each day, more than 90 Americans die prematurely from an overdose that involves an opioid[11]. From

---

shrinking and may no longer be the majority religion within just a few decades, research finds," 12 September 2022, https://www.cbsnews.com/news/christianity-us-shrinking-pew-research/
[9] ibid
[10] Editors Jonathan K. Phillips, Morgan A. Ford, and Richard J. Bonnie, National Library of Medicine: National Center for Biotechnology Information, "Pain Management and the Opioid Epidemic: Balancing Societal and Individual Benefits and Risks of Prescription Opioid Use," 13 July 2017, https://www.ncbi.nlm.nih.gov/books/NBK458661/
[11] American Society of Anesthesiologists, "Opioid Abuse," (Date Extracted) 1 March 2023, https://www.asahq.org/madeforthismoment/pain-management/opioid-treatment/opioid-abuse

1999 to 2011, hydrocodone use increased more than two-fold, oxycodone use increased by more than five-fold, and the mortality rate of opioid-related overdose almost four-fold[12]. This is a massive problem that most people are overlooking. Whole swaths of the country are being hollowed out and killed by painkillers and pill-pushers.

Problems in the United States don't get solved, they get compounded. The War on Poverty was a pipedream. The War on Drugs was lost, and drug deaths are worse than before. Meanwhile, the War on Terrorism remains an eternal procession of flag draped coffins courtesy of the Graveyard of Empires.

The opioid epidemic will not be solved, it can't be solved within the current political system. Pill-mills will be shut down and dealers will certainly be caught, but no full measures will be

[12] Editors Jonathan K. Phillips, Morgan A. Ford, and Richard J. Bonnie, National Library of Medicine: National Center for Biotechnology Information, "Pain Management and the Opioid Epidemic: Balancing Societal and Individual Benefits and Risks of Prescription Opioid Use," 13 July 2017, https://www.ncbi.nlm.nih.gov/books/NBK458661/

implemented to solve the problem. We are a country of half-measures or no-measures. Mr. American, forget the problem until your nephew overdoses in his friend's basement.

Roughly two out of three U.S. adults are overweight or obese (69%) and one out of three are obese (36%) per the Harvard School of Public Health[13]. Although, obesity rates are higher in black, Hispanic, and Mexican American adults than in White adults. If Americanism trends continue, by 2030, estimates predict that roughly half of all men and women will be obese. That obesity trend should also not be surprising, since the CDC recorded that nearly 37% of American adults[14] consumed fast food on a given day (that is from 2016 data). Moreover, 83% of American families eat at fast

---

[13] Harvard University, T.F. Chan School of Public Health, "Obesity Prevention Source," (extracted 19 February 2023), https://www.hsph.harvard.edu/obesity-prevention-source/obesity-trends-original/obesity-rates-worldwide/

[14] National Safety Council, Safety & Health, "Nearly 37 percent of Americans regularly eat fast food, study shows," 6 December 2018, https://www.safetyandhealthmagazine.com/articles/17784-nearly-37-percent-of-americans-regularly-eat-fast-food-study-shows#

food restaurants at least once a week[15], which would help explain why approximately 20% of American children and adolescents are obese[16].

Not only does American culture create overweight, illiterate nincompoops, but they're also divorced from their own family history. Ancestry.com and OnePoll discovered through their survey research that 34% of Americans cannot trace their family tree past their grandparents, and a third of them couldn't even name all four of their grandparents[17]. A fifth of survey participants (21%) were unable to name just one of their great-grandparents[18]. So, when a crusty Twitter leftist attempts to describe their great-grandfather (who landed at Anzio beachhead, for example) as an

---

[15] Jacqueline Howard, CNN, "Here's how much fast food Americans are eating," 3 October 2018, https://edition.cnn.com/2018/10/03/health/fast-food-consumption-cdc-study/index.html
[16] Center for Disease Control and Prevention, Data & Statistics, "Childhood Obesity Facts," (extracted 19 February 2023), https://www.cdc.gov/obesity/data/childhood.html
[17] Nicola Haslam, New York Post, "One-third of Americans can't name all of their grandparents," 19 December 2018, https://nypost.com/2018/12/19/one-third-of-americans-cant-name-all-of-their-grandparents/
[18] ibid

"antifascist," please realize that they very likely do not even know his name or what city he was born in.

The old American culture encouraged thrifty behavior and protecting one's savings – usually to ensure that families created generational wealth. That is no longer the case with Americanism, and this is for good reason: the American Empire wants its subjects in debt and poor. This is facilitated within the modern culture and under the guise of "consumerism." As of September 2022, American consumer debt was at $16.5 trillion, with the average American consumer debt at $96,371[19]. The overall debt figure includes credit card balances, student loans, mortgages, etc. Credit card debt increased by almost $85 billion by the end of the fourth quarter of 2022, the biggest quarterly increase ever, according to WalletHub[20]. This was

---

[19] Lane Gillespie, Bankrate, "Average American debt statistics," 13 January 2023, https://www.bankrate.com/personal-finance/debt/average-american-debt/

[20] Alina Comoreanu, WalletHub, "Credit Card Debt Study," 8 March 2023, https://wallethub.com/edu/cc/credit-card-debt-study/24400

the largest year-over-year increase in more than 20 years. Again, not sustainable, and certainly not beneficial to the American citizenry, especially the Southern people.

Unfortunately, we're not a serious country. We're not serious, we're consumers. The credit card is our plastic ticket for trinkets and trips. Whereas our grandfathers were frugal, we're flippant with money (really, just debt). We don't make tangible things anymore, we make transactions, interest rates, and listen to "Please Hold." Debt slavery is more real than any fabrication of White Privilege Theory – and it hurts everyone. It is not a bug, it's a feature in a consumer-centered economy. That's the way Uncle Sam likes it.

Nielsen Soundscan's 2018 year-end music industry report confirmed that R&B/hip-hop was the most popular genre of music in America. Nine out of the ten most popular "songs" in the American Empire were hip-hop/R&B songs; and as streaming has become the dominant form to consume music, eight of the ten most streamed "musicians" were rappers[21]. For most normal, traditional Southerners, hip-hop/R&B/rap (whatever you want to call it) is not the musical genre of choice. However, within the realm of Americanism, this type of music, if one can even describe it as such, rules the day. In 2020, rapper Cardi B's number-one single "WAP" (an acronym for something that cannot be published) debuted atop the U.S. *Billboard Hot* 100 and had the largest opening streaming week for a song in American history[22]. From a lyrical perspective, it is not fit to print. With respect to music, is this the direction we want to proceed for our Southern children and families? If we remain under Americanism, we will not have a choice in the matter.

---

[21] Insanul Ahmed, Billboard, "Is Hip-Hop's Dominance Slipping? 'My Concern Is the Magic Is Gone'," 18 October 2022, https://www.billboard.com/pro/hip-hop-music-most-popular-genre-dominance-slipping/

[22] Gary Trust, Billboard, "Cardi B & Megan Thee Stallion's 'WAP' Debuts at No. 1 on Billboard Hot 100 With Record First-Week Streams," 17 August 2020, https://www.billboard.com/pro/cardi-bs-wap-debuts-no-1-hot-100/

The vulgarity and coarseness that is at the heart of Cardi B's putrid output is representative of a larger trend of debased crassness that is systemic and rampant throughout Americanism. A study from 2017[23] reviewed the tendency in the usage of the late George Carlin's "seven words you can never say on television" in American books from 1950 to 2008. The study revealed an unvarying increase in the use of curse words. Ironically, Carlin was himself a proponent in our national downturn into barbaric discourse.

Moreover, and this should not come as a shock to Southern dissidents, the study found that books published between 2005 to 2008 were 28 times more likely to include foul language than books published in the early 1950s; the increases for individual swear words ranged from 4 to 678 times![24]

---

[23] Jean M. Twenge, Hannah VanLandingham, and W. Keith Campbell, <u>San Diego State Unniversity and the University of Georgia</u>, 3 August 2017, "The Seven Words You Can Never Say on Television: Increases in the Use of Swear Words in American Books, 1950-2008," https://journals.sagepub.com/doi/pdf/10.1177/2158244017723689

[24] ibid

Noticing trends can get rightwing dissidents in a great deal of trouble in modern America. Americanism's commitment to linguistic humiliation is one that will continue, especially when paired with the Empire's declining domestic educational programs and its prevailing culture.

If Americanism is corrupting books with foul language, what about television? If you're reading this essay, and haven't been living under a rock, you can probable already take a guess that this medium of entertainment is also aligned with American degeneracy. In 2005 and 2010 (those years almost seem quaint by comparison to today), the Parents Television Council ("PTC") conducted reviews regarding curse words and expletives used during prime-time television. Per the PTC: "Across all networks use of profanity on prime-time broadcast entertainment programming increased 69.3% from 2005 to 2010." On top of that, the PTC determined that the most popular curse word on television was the (bleeped) F-word; it found 156 instances of the word, compared to a single instance in 2005[25]. Of course, one only needs to watch current American television (I do not recommend this for your sanity and soul) to observe the stark decline in quality, but also the increased deterioration in language.

Unfortunately, swearing on television is not the only malady we have to contend with. Even back in 2013[26] the PTC was reporting, "that blurred or pixilated full nudity is increasingly being shown on prime-time broadcast television shows, and that almost 70% of this type of nudity is being shown on TV-PG rated programs." The PTC[27] also determined that NBC and ABC were the most responsible, with those networks accounting "for 88% of the full nudity that aired on prime-time broadcast television." Needless to say, this

---

[25] Lindsay Powers and Georg Szalai, The Hollywood Reporter, "Parents Television Council: TV Profanity Has Increased 69% in Five Years," 9 November 2010, Parents Television Council: TV Profanity Has Increased 69% in Five Years – The Hollywood Reporter
[26] Whitney Friedlander, Variety, "TV Nudity On the Rise: Study," 4 June 2013, https://variety.com/2013/tv/news/nudity-on-broadcast-tv-modern-family-parks-and-rec-1200492331/
[27] ibid

information was from several years ago and does not include many of the more recent promoters of nudity on television, such as HBO, Showtime, and Starz. Their products now include full frontal male and female nudity, as well as graphic heterosexual intercourse and "other" sex acts. All of it, regrettably, readily available for most American and Southern children to consume.

The rise of nudity and sexualism on prime-time and premium television is a lamentable segue to another seedier component of Americanism: pornography and American addiction. According to The Recovery Village's Pornography Statistics and Facts[28], porn addiction, or problematic pornography usage, affects approximately 3% to 10% of the U.S. adult population. Sadly, the median age of first exposure to pornography is now only 14 years old, although it is my summation that the age of exposure will likely decrease with the increase in

---

[28] Dr. Jessica Pyhtila and Jonathan Strum, The Recovery Village, "Pornography Statistics and Facts," 13 September 2022, https://www.therecoveryvillage.com/process-addiction/porn-addiction/pornography-statistics/

availability of entertainment supplied nudity and sexualism and the widespread accessibility of porn. Also sobering is that, up to 65% of young adult men and 18% of young women report watching porn *at least* once a week[29]. When it reaches 100% on a daily basis, will we realize that Americanism is actually harmful? An entire book could be dedicated to the dangerous effects of porn usage and addiction, this mere paragraph is only designed to provide another melancholy illumination regarding Americanism's dismal track record.

Like a snake eating its own tail, the promotion of Americanism has also significantly reduced American patriotism within the Empire. Of course, engaging in endless wars, including an embarrassing withdrawal from Afghanistan, and the widespread destruction of American and Southern history and public monuments, will naturally reduce patriotic fervor. Per Gallup polling[30], before 2015,

---

[29] University of Texas – Dallas, Student Counseling Center, "Pornography Addiction," (extracted 9 March 2023), https://counseling.utdallas.edu/pornaddiction/
[30] Megan Brenan, Gallup, "Record-Low 38% Extremely Proud to Be American," 29 June 2022,

no less than 55% of American adults said they were extremely proud of the United States. The highest readings followed the 9/11 terrorist attacks, when American patriotism surged. Nonetheless, extreme national pride in America has been sliding since 2015, falling below the majority level in 2018; as of 2022, it is nearly 20 points lower than it was a decade ago. For Southern Nationalists, we must encourage this decline in misplaced patriotism. Americans seem to understand that something is radically off about modern America, and that Americanism is a poison pill designed to harm the patient, the American citizenry. It is our mission, as Southern Nationalists, to escape the hospital before Americanism euthanizes our people.

*****

There are an almost endless number of other issues that can be explored regarding the depravity of Americanism. However, the critical component is the Southern people, and Dixian culture, chained to

---

https://news.gallup.com/poll/394202/record-low-extremely-proud-american.aspx

the Leviathan on the Potomac. Its appetite is insatiable; it will, given another generation of unrelenting progress, destroy our culture until nothing is left, except Americanism. Peaceful, political secession is the only recourse to save our Southern children from being groomed, to keep our churches faithful to the Bible, to continuing hearing Southern accents, to restore financial sanity, and to carry on with civilization.

Push for secession at every opportunity. For if we fail, our posterity will not identify as Southerners – instead, they'll be something else entirely. They'll be modern Americans, and we perish the thought.

About the Author: Rick Dirtwater (pseudonym) is a High Church Episcopalian and hails from Virginia's Tidewater region. His ancestors were in the House of Burgesses, and he is also related to one of the South's most ardent "Lost Causers," General Jubal Early. He is a devoted husband and father. He can be found somewhere east of Virginia's Fall Line, enjoying Chesapeake blue crabs, fried oysters, and bourbon.

Adversaries of the South: The Left's Failed Elites, *By Harmonica*

One of the most significant challenges Southern Nationalists faces, especially in the past five to six years, has been the threat of doxing: the publishing of one's personal information online, particularly in regard to one's political views, with the goal of getting the target terminated from their job and subjected to ongoing harassment. This threat is why it is a good idea to use a pseudonym. Many people have had their careers destroyed in a single instance. An untold number of others, although holding pro-Southern and traditionalist viewpoints, have opted to stay on the sidelines, fearing what would happen if they were doxed. It does not matter how low ranking the job may be. There have been pizza delivery drivers terminated for their political views. I feel confident in stating that doxing is the single biggest threat to the Dissident Right and the Southern Nationalist movement, and the critical explanation as to why we have stagnated as a movement.

Though the Dissident Right has spilled a lot of ink on *how* to avoid being doxed, something it lacks is a comprehensive understanding as to *why* doxings happen, beyond simple leftwing vindictiveness. Understanding what motivates leftwing doxing is essential to understanding the mentality behind it, why radical leftists are so hellbent to ruin lives, and, as such, provide the Dissident Right and Southern Nationalists a better understanding of what we are up against, and why the Left is so dangerous on this point.

Russian-American scholar Peter Turchin has come up with the best theory as to why the doxings are happening and continue to occur, although he has not, to my knowledge, applied his theoretical framework to the current order, at least, in so far as it relates to modern doxing as a tactic. Turchin's theory, laid out most succinctly in his *War and Peace and War, Secular Cycles*, and *Ages of Discord*, examines how societies go through the "good times-bad times" cycle. At the time of this writing, Turchin is one of my favorite living scholars, and he has developed a rich and complex theory that does a fantastic job of explaining societal shifts and why all societies eventually devolve into conflict. Turchin's theory is highly complex and does a wonderful job explaining why these United States appears to be heading toward major social collapse and political disunion.

Here is a concise version of Turchin's theory: building off the work of Islamic scholar Ibn Khaldun, Turchin states that societies that face a great number of hardships will develop a fighting spirit, a notion of collective solidarity which Khaldun called *asabiyyah* (Arabic for "group feeling" or "social cohesion"). Nations on the edge of a wider civilization are particularly prone to develop *asabiyyah*, as they are well acquainted with nations wildly different from them; hence, why Macedonia and Rome, both nations on the edge of the wider Mediterranean-based classical civilizations, were able to form great empires. In more recent times, we have observed this same trend in Spain and the Ottoman Empire, as both nations were on the edge between Christian and Islamic civilizations. More recently, we witnessed with these United States, a nation (or better put, a collection of nations) sitting as a Western outpost against the American Indian Tribes. However, with great success comes eventual decline, as the *asabiyyah* that allows nations to form powerful empires eventually causes them to become wealthy and decadent. Eventually these nations lose their fighting spirit and, finally, their empire dissolves.

The reasons for the loss of *asabiyyah* are multi-casual. There is no single magic bullet to explain this trend. However, for the sake of brevity, only one aspect of Turchin's theory will be utilized in this essay, as this element is most important in comprehending why the Left brandishes doxing as a weapon against their political opponents. This critical aspect of Turchin's theory is entitled "elite overproduction."

According to Turchin, one of the best indicators that a society is headed toward major strife is when it suffers from elite overproduction. Essentially, it is when a society produces too many elites than allotted roles to accommodate their numbers. A large group of failed elites are created. These are people who believe they should be *elite* but are, for various reasons, unable to remain in that socioeconomic stratum. Consequently, they attempt to destroy their competition, creating spaces they hope to fill. Per Turchin, elite overproduction was epidemic in the last days of the Roman Empire, as well as France during the French Wars of Religion. Additionally, an uptick in dueling can be linked to elite overproduction.

Elite overproduction was a major problem during the last days of Tsarist Russia. Turchin has come up with a theoretical framework to explain why the Russian Revolution was not made by poverty-stricken peasants and industrial workers, as Marx had predicted. Rather, the former remained staunchly Tsarist until the badly mishandled (by everyone involved) Bloody Sunday in 1905. Instead, the Revolution was spearheaded by the children of prominent families. For example, Lenin's father was the superintendent of the Saint Petersburg school system, while Sophia Perovskaya, Vera Figner, and Ignacy Hryniewiecki, three of the assassins of Tsar Alexander II, came from aristocratic families. By applying elite overproduction to late Tsarist Russia, Turchin has solved one of the biggest puzzles of Russian history: why the Tsarist regime was brought down by its own elites. In that same fashion, Turchin's model offers valuable insights into the nature of the Western antifa (America and Europe) and why they are attracted to such an ideology. Similar to late period Russia, rural people and the working class have limited interests in leftist ideologies, instead it is the domain of the college educated professional class, or those that have the credentials to enter that class. Furthermore, many of them do, in fact, come from wealthy families.

With Turchin's theory in mind, we understand the nature of doxings - it is the failed elites lashing out. Consider the stereotypical antifa member, or hyper-liberal woman, that adores ratting out strangers in the hope of getting them terminated from their jobs. They are typically college educated, often with a post-graduate degree(s), but are underemployed, often well below their own expectations. By discovering people and then prompting their termination and unemployment, antifa-types are hoping to take out potential rival elites and clear a space for themselves. In turn, they can achieve the elite status to which they feel entitled. Remember, leftists do not really mind hierarchy per se, they just need to be at the top of that hierarchy. Hence the Soviet Union very quickly developed into a polity governed by Communist Party elites, who would then use their own connections to furnish for themselves "elite" and lavish lifestyles, despite all the claims that they were building an egalitarian workers' paradise.

There is a reason why Marxism appeals to low paid intellectuals. Marxism inevitably leads to a technocratic dictatorship thanks to the complexities in centrally running a nation's economy, and they view themselves as having the skills to rule under this new order. The Marxist dream of a centrally planned economy is just that, a dream. The economy is too complex and has too many variables for a single planning agency to capture and manage. Fredrich Hayek was correct about the knowledge problem. But to what extent it "works" or, perhaps better put, "functions" – requires technocrats. With such a need, a cabal of technocrats and academics seek such a system within which they can thrive.

Throughout history, failed elites have tried a variety of methods to obtain the status they believe has been unfairly denied to them. One of the more fascinating aspects of Turchin's work is that he illustrates how elite overproduction is a major driving force behind dueling. For all the rhetoric about "honor" (and I am fully aware of the topic within the greater framework of Southern

Nationalism) it is worth remembering that dead people cannot compete for elite positions; furthermore, when one is faced with the prospects of the humiliation of being a failed elite, the risks inherent in dueling becomes worth the risk. But Marxism, with its advocacy of central planning and the technocratic class that must arise from it, is particularly attractive to the failed elites.

For the failed elites of the early 21st Century, "Wokism" is even more attractive than classical Marxism. Think of the ever-changing jargon that exists within the Far Left. A single word or phrase can go from acceptable to inexcusable almost overnight. To become the new elite in such a system requires an almost obsessive attachment, one that the casual person, with hobbies, interests, and responsibilities, will not be able to manage. Keeping up within the new Left's linguistic minefield created by the would-be new elites is far too exhausting for a normal citizen. They are, in essence, crafting a system tailor-made to allow them to rule, as it will exclude any other potential elites, not only from the Right but from the mainstream Left. Ultimately, their rule can be unchallenged because linguistic hegemony.

Additionally, do not be deceived by their egalitarian rhetoric. They desire to rule and want a system that will allow them to place themselves over others. This is what the Left has always done. Although there are some differences between the Radical Left of the 1960/70s and the Radical Left of today, there are enough parallels between them to make a study of that earlier leftism to understand the radicals of today. First off, and most obvious, the cultural changes the Left obtained, even with the various conservative backlashes, set the stage for the modern Left. For example, the Left's victory in legalizing contraception in the 1960s was the sexual liberation catalyst for the eventual acceptance of homosexual marriage. Homosexual marriage led to the emergence of transgenderism as a political ideology versus a personal position.

As it is today, the Left of the 1960s were also the children of the elites, becoming the backbone of hardcore leftwing groups. A review of the Harvard Students for Democratic Society ("SDS"), the most important of the radical 1960s organizations, revealed that they were not the intelligent, aspirational students who entered Harvard by their own merits, but rather the legacy admissions. In other words, the students of the Harvard SDS came from the upper class – the elites.

The SDS also presents an opportunity to observe what leftwing radicals from wealthy backgrounds eventually want to achieve: transform themselves into a new elite, even at the expense of their own followers. In 1969, a radical group of students at the University of Michigan-Ann Arbor split from the national organization, considering their parent organization as too timid, and launched a terrorist campaign. That group would be influenced by the Bob Dylan song "Subterranean Homesick Blues" and dub themselves the Weathermen (specifically, from the lyric, "You don't need to be a weatherman to know which way the wind blows"). In and of itself, the Weathermen (eventually renamed the "Weather Underground Organization" after the original name was deemed "sexist") is a fascinating case study of failed elites and radicalized rich kids. The leaders of the organization, Bill Ayers and Bernadine Dohrn, were both privileged children from wealthy Upper Midwest (Yankee) families.

The Weathermen serves as a case study in the desire of leftwing radicals to set themselves up as the new elite as soon as they take power. In the case of the Weathermen, they did not even wait until they took power. After they began their bombing campaign, the Weathermen went underground so they could continue their crusade. Here is where their story gets interesting. While the lower ranking members of the organization were cramped together in slums, Ayers and Dorhn did not share this fate. Rather, they lived in a spacious waterfront property while they waged war against these United States and capitalism. Both were worried that they would not be able to maintain the elite status they were born into, and one to which they felt entitled. Consequently, they turned to Marxism in the hopes they would be able to obtain that elite status they dreamed of. Of course, the use of egalitarian rhetoric was just a cover.

There are many parallels one can draw between the "Era of Turmoil" (roughly 1964-1979) and especially its most violent years between 1967-1970, when it appeared as if the country was on the verge of a civil war, and today. But one difference does stand out: the problem of elite overproduction is even worse now thanks, in large part, to globalism. The aspiring elite of the late 1960s really only had to compete with the people within their own nation. The aspiring global elite of today must compete with the world, and that means there will be more failed elites. The number of elites has increased tremendously while the number of elite positions has stayed largely stagnant. It is no wonder so many eager elites are turning to a system which, if put into practice, would allow them to obtain the elite positions they seek: arbiters of global society. In effect, they wish to become rulers by weaponizing speech and regulate thought. For them, the choice is stark – create a system that will allow you to become an elite or fail.

It may be true that many low paid and decidedly non-elite people have been fired from their jobs. As has already been mentioned, this includes pizza delivery drivers. But the pizza delivery driver is simply collateral damage. The real target is not the pizza delivery man, but the business owner who must bend the knee or lose his business. It is a humiliation ritual and one that is done to prove their power over a small business owner.

Still, the greatest targets are people whom the Far Left considers as their genuine competition. Service industry employees might be at risk, but far and away the greater threat comes from the Dissident Right, including Southern Nationalists, employed in the corporate world and, even more so, in academia. These individuals, advocates for civilization, Christianity, and tradition. They enjoy careers that the stereotypical antifa member desperately desires and is willing to "take them out" to get it. Dueling is certainly more honorable than anonymously reporting someone for "wrong think," but the impulse behind both practices is similar.

The Dissident Right's higher functioning members tend to be psychologically and socially stable individuals with significant skillsets that leftists lack. Numerous psychological studies have indicated that leftists tend to suffer from greater rates of depression, suicidal thoughts, and mental anguish than their counterparts on the political right. They are also drawn toward different skillsets. Very few members of the antifa derive from backgrounds that include training in business, economics, finance, or the hard sciences. Consequently, they cannot bring to the table the necessary capacity to contribute to a less forgiving capitalist business landscape. They derive from academic disciplines grounded in nuance and emotion, such as the social sciences or liberal arts, that provide few technical skills. In order to compete, leftwing failed elites not only have to target their counterparts in the Dissident Right, but they must also change the meaning of business itself. No longer is profit the motivating factor; rather, a social good becomes the goal of the financial enterprise. This is necessary to make their inferior studies and interests relevant.

Correspondingly, as much as the Dissident Right is at threat in both the corporate and academic world, the antifa is also going after solid liberals more aggressively. Again, they are eliminating competition. This explains why the list of "offenses" will continue to grow longer. They need to eliminate more and more competition. Thus, the goal post needs to move further and further to the left. Of course, there are very few elites in the corporate world who have anything close to Dissident Right or Southern Nationalist views. Therefore, targeting our people can only go so far. The Left must cannibalize itself to make space for the failed elites.

The entertainment industry bears this out. No one would accuse comedian Dave Chappelle, or Trey Parker and Matt Stone, the creators of *South Park,* for rightwing ideologues. Yet, that is the label they earned by their lack of conforming to new values. It was not that long ago that transgressive comedians like *Monty Python* or *South Park* were openly joking about the mental illness of transsexuals. That was a position deemed uncontroversial. Today, uttering such a progressive heresy will cost someone their job – as it did with Chappelle (albeit, briefly).

Above all else, there is one thing Southern Nationalists must understand about the behavior of the Far Left. Snitching on someone for their political opinions to a corporate Twitter account for wrong think is many things – cowardly, juvenile, underhanded, and wicked. It is the actions of a lesser person, one who is willing to callously condemn someone to potential poverty and harassment, including innocent children. It is one of the most dishonorable things someone can do. However, doxing is not irrational. Doxing, as evil as it is, is understandable in so far as other potential elites are now unemployable. In that sense, it is rational and effective, much as it stands to reason that the nobles of Old Europe, fearing their loss of status, would begin to challenge their fellow nobles to a duel over an insult or verbal slight. Did that come with great risk? Of course, occasionally the person that made that initial challenge would be killed in combat. But it was seen by many as a worthy risk, especially in an era of elite overproduction. During the time of dueling, the potential elite faced a serious dilemma: kill off competitors or face the humiliation of becoming a failed elite.

The potential elite have a great deal of their identity tied up in their status. To lose that status is the loss of their very identity. There is a reason why so many of the lower nobility found themselves so deeply in debt, some to the point where they were eventually forced to sell off their titles to survive. They wanted to maintain, at least superficially, the appearance of that elite status. With that in mind, it can now be better understood why so many of them resorted to dueling. It is the same mindset that would often lead to inter-noble civil war, such as in the English War of the Roses and French Wars of Religion. During both of those time periods, England and France were suffering from a high degree of elite overproduction, and it was becoming much more difficult for potential elites to obtain and maintain their status. Wars in which the nobility killed each other off became a solution to that problem. Inter-nobility strife meant fewer potential elites, thus the potential elites that survived had an easier time remaining within their respective societal positions.

History has patterns, and much as the failed elites of Old Europe would use certain tactics to eliminate their competition, such as dueling, the failed elites of late period Tsarist Russia used Bolshevism to liquidate their competition. Failed elites in a declining America have turned to "Wokism." Doxing is merely the means to remove their competition. Thus, the Dissident Right and Southern Nationalists must take the Far Left with the utmost seriousness. The Left is comprised of desperate people. They are, psychologically, in a life and death struggle for their identity.

Many of the antifa typically have college degrees from elite schools. Some have advanced degrees. Yet, they have little to show for it. They can frequently be found working at a dead-end job or as an underemployed journalist. Any hope they have of escaping their situation relies on becoming elites, but due to an overproduction of potential elites, this is becoming increasingly difficult. Doxing and destroying the careers of rightwing dissidents becomes a rational, if immoral, solution to this problem.

Underlying all of this is the success antifa and the Far Left enjoys – they have the ideological backing of the vast majority of Corporate America and have for at least a decade. I can remember the reaction of the center Right, namely from Ben Shapiro and others, when "Wokism" first began to emerge from certain academic departments and creeped into the mainstream around 2011 or 2012. Shapiro, and other ineffective "conservatives" like him, thought this new brand of political correctness was as ridiculous as everyone else. Their ultimate attitude was one of dismissal. Shapiro, in particular, argued that the appeal of "Wokism" was simply an identity attachment for college-aged radicals, and the universities they attended were encouraging it. But, as the argument went, eventually these leftists would graduate and be forced to get a real job in "the real world." The belief was that these silly ideas would die on the vine as the private sector would not entertain such delusional fantasies. A few conservative commentators even speculated that "Feminist Studies" and other related majors would be worse than useless on a job application. Needless to say, that flippant attitude regarding "Wokism" was wrong. Instead of being blunted by the real world, the Far Left's burgeoning, rabid hatred of all things White, Southern, and Christian took over the institutions (public and private). In turn, the leftist radicals declared another campaign in the culture war on Heritage America and Dixie.

I do not want to be overly critical of the center Right. No one owns a crystal ball and I do not think any honest observer would admit that they thought the Left would achieve this level of success. Many of those now within the Dissident Right and the Southern Nationalist movement held a similar viewpoint in 2011. I believed the leftist radicals were the object of pure mockery rather than a force that would rapidly take over almost every major institution within a few years. Not just within the halls of academia from which they sprang, but also almost all major corporations, the majority of mainline religious institutions, and even the United States military – once a bedrock of rightwing and Southern values. However plausible mainstream conservative thinking may have been a decade ago, it did not pan out. There was an extremely successful leftist takeover of practically all American institutions. Now, we must adjust to this new reality.

Previously mainstream liberal elites have typically said something in the past that could get them "cancelled" and permanently unemployed. As the goal posts continue to move, the current occupants of liberal elite status will become collaborators as a survival mechanism. Such liberals are hoping to fend off the radicals and continue to keep their own positions, if that requires turning a blind eye as their friends and family members are ruined through doxing, then so be it. Certain segments of the non-Bolshevik Russian elite tried to do the same thing. They failed, as will the current crop of American elites trying to satisfy the antifa's increasingly extreme demands. This is, of course, about a great deal more than just opposing "fascism" (the Far Left's catchall term for anything considered healthy and normal only a decade ago).

While capacity envy is certainly a major factor, one of the foundational elements of antifa's desire to purge America and the South is the constant urge to destroy what great men of the past have built. It reminds them of their own dismal failures. Failed elites can and certainly will cripple nations. They are envious of those that have what they do not, and they are willing to destroy any reminders of their inabilities to get power. When you read about someone who was fired for their political views, be they Dissident Right, a Southern Nationalist, or a mainstream liberal, you are witnessing a spot opening up for some antifa member to take that position, bringing themselves one step closer to solidifying their rule.

Turchin's theory of elite overproduction adequately explains the cycles of several historical societies – Ancient Rome, Medieval England and France, and Tsarist Russia. His theory also has tremendous explaining power for understanding the current state and decline of these United States. The theory is multi-faceted, and his work demands to be read to fully appreciate our current predicament. The theory is of particular importance because it explains why the children of the wealthy are so often drawn to radical leftwing politics, a trend that has come up time and time again in vastly different societies. It should be of specific interest to the Dissident Right and Southern Nationalists, as it does a fantastic job explaining why the Left has undertaken doxing as an effective tactic.

By comprehending elite overproduction, and the dangerous failed elites it creates, we can observe that, to the Far Left, this is a life and death struggle. Not because leftists think they are preventing another Holocaust. Rather, they know they are in danger of becoming failed elites and have launched a campaign to destroy the careers of their competition. With that competition now unemployable, they hope that those elite positions open to them.

There may be differences, but this is the same tactic failed elites have taken throughout history. It is cowardly and evil, but it is not irrational. The Dissident Right and Southern Nationalists must come to terms with the driving motivation of doxing. In 1917, failed elites managed to destroy Tsarist Russia, placing that nation under Bolshevik tyranny for several bloody, inhuman decades. Russia is only just starting to recover from that nightmare. Even then, the recovery is slow and uneven. Communism, in all of its forms, has a way of destroying societies. "Wokism" will offer the same fate to nations that fall under its rule. This is what is at stake in these United States and our South, thanks to a new batch of failed elites.

We cannot let them win.

About the Author: Harmonica (pseudonym) is a son of the Deep South with the blood of Anglo-Celtic warriors running through his veins. He has been drawn to Dixie and her cause since early childhood, having been influenced by the stories of the Confederate brave spun by his grandmother. As a boy he swore to God that he would dedicate his life to freeing his people. He has kept that promise. Harmonica is a successful surgeon in a large urban location within the South that is affiliated with a university – thus, his personal knowledge of having witnessed failed elites in action. He has a wife and four small children, all of whom are under the age of ten.

Is the Orthodox Faith the Solution? Building Upon a Southern Ethnos Through True Faith,
By Rebecca Dillingham

"The South, many believe, still has a substantial authentic culture, both high and folk, and it still has a purchase on Christianity. That is, the South is a civilizational reality in a sense which the United States is not, and it will last longer than the American Empire." – Dr. Clyde Wilson

America's a goner, y'all. Simply put, you cannot save "a nation" which has no "national" attributes. The United States has become a managerial state, an administrative behemoth with no geographical, geopolitical, or moral constraints. It is an amorphous blob compromised of polyglot territories cobbled together by secular fictions, utopian fantasies, consumerism, covetousness, degeneracy, and hubris. Yet, the South is distinct.

Although we find ourselves within the geography of these United States, Dixie has many of the attributes one would seek in "a nation." Thus, one area that requires exploration is the South's religious identity. It is both critical to the regional zeitgeist and simultaneously problematic. The South's unique relationship with Christianity provides a limited defense of the South from the grotesque immorality of the rest of the other members of these United States. However, the disjointed nature of the South's Christian identity harms the cultural fabric of the South itself, in many ways eroding its ability to combat a depraved "American" ideology. The South must find a balance between its own cultural needs and a united Christian vision in order to combat federal interpretations of "national identity."

In fact, America's godless gargantuan and obsessive multiculturalism are in direct contradiction with what even makes "a nation": borders, language, and culture. These distinctions create a society, and it's from those tangible building blocks that "a people" come into being. But that noble birth is only part of the civilizational battle. Sustenance and protection are also required.

The "American *ethnos*," says political analyst Jim Jatras, was "characterized by European ancestry, by the English language, and by the Christian religion, mostly Protestant." A nation cannot be a theoretical idea, an ideal, or a proposition. It's organic and cannot be created or forced by sheer will of man.

"The constitutional order established by the Founding Fathers… for themselves and their posterity is a secondary epiphenomenon, the *ethos* of the founding *ethnos*, their folkways and values," continued Jatras. "The primary phenomenon, without which the erstwhile constitutional order would not have existed in the first place, from which it derived its values, principles, and structure, is the ethnos. *That* is what is under attack, even more than the order itself, which in my opinion is effectively gone."

I would argue, though, that his defined "ethnos" never really existed in "America" at large, even from its earliest days. Certainly not in colonial times. Settlements were expressly unique and diverse from one another. Each was overwhelmingly homogeneous in social order, language, and even religion. After the Revolution, each colony then became a sovereign within a confederation of *these* "United States." Like the cantons of Switzerland, every state became a "nation" unto itself, with their own common ethnos and varying degrees of self-governing communities and small-scale living.

When a supposedly new and improved federalist system was agreed upon through a Convention of States in 1787, "America" *still* remained a voluntary entity comprised of many independent entities. Referring to their distinct nature, Thomas Jefferson called the states, "Empires of Liberty." Each acceded individually to what they all hoped (save for a few big-government subversives) would be a mutually beneficial contract.

Therefore, "America" was still no nation and most definitely had no ethnos. When atheist Abraham Lincoln pandered to voters in 1858 and uttered, "A house divided against itself cannot stand," the stealthy politician was telling a lie.

Despite the truthfulness of the New Testament verse he quoted, America was never "a house" in the cohesive "nation" sense of the word. It was better viewed as a town with many separate houses.

"It has been [America's] fate not to have an ideology, but to be one."— Richard Hofstadter

Regardless, the idea of Unionism was strong throughout the early to mid-19th Century. Interestingly, according to historian Dr. John Devanny, "it was Southerners who embraced the great national wars against Great Britain in 1812 and Mexico in the 1840s… [and] the concepts of national greatness and manifest destiny." Sure, there had been talk of secession as early as the 1790s and even most zealously among some statesmen in the North, but the illusion of unity within a decentralist republic was fully realized with the presidential election of 1860. It was the tipping point that gave the South a "national consciousness." Then, through blood and fire, Dixie was further forged into a real identity making her "the first 'captive nation' of the Yankee Empire," as described by the Kennedy brothers, authors of the recommended *The South Was Right!*

There was much else that cultivated Dixie's nationalist roots. Fugitive poet and Southern Agrarian Allen Tate said that prior to the War, the South was America's only European civilizational order, rooted in both the material of soil (agriculture) but the non-material of virtue, duty, and honor (order and hierarchy). Preeminent Southern historian, Dr. Clyde Wilson, contends that still now "Southern culture is a product of the high point of Western civilization" – the fruition of hundreds of years of British Common Law heritage, language, literature, art, social mores, and a Christian "ethos."

However, Tate bemoaned that even though there was a "common historical myth" and "a religious life" among Southerners, their Christianity was so utterly disorganized that it "was not powerfully united to the religious experience, as it was in medieval society." Although "a feudal society" with customs stemming from a biblical moral code, asserted Tate, Dixie was "without a feudal religion" and its "religious mind was inarticulate, dissenting, and schismatical." In fact, this Southern stalwart considered confused religiosity to be the main contributor to Dixie's devastating defeat – militarily, culturally, and existentially.

"The South did not adopt an agricultural and hierarchical religion to support its civilization," writer Gary Potter commented. "Even the 'High Church' Episcopalianism exemplified by Bishop [Leonidas] Polk and embraced by President [Jefferson] Davis was not very widely practiced by ordinary Southerners. Instead, too much of the South adopted, as Tate puts it, 'the Teutonic Puritanism of the New England textile manufacturers.'"

Philosopher Dr. Clark Carlton echoed, "Tate observed that Southerners developed a sacramental view of the places and life of the South [the grace of God working in concert with creation and for our redemption] but, being largely Protestant, did not have a sacramental religion [no Eucharist, no Holy Mysteries]." This concept was explored further. "The result was tragic," Potter added. "Without the right religion to support and sustain its civilization, the South, it can be said, lost the War Between the States even before the first shots were fired." In other words, the South with its varied forms of Christianity could not withstand the spiritual and physical assault of the Yankee Empire during the War, much less in the aftermath of hellish reconstruction and counterfeit reconciliation. As blogger Walt Garlington aptly surmised: And "the South has been at odds with herself since."

The postbellum South has become even more disjointed and has been called many things: "Christ haunted" by Flannery O'Connor and "peculiarly Christian" by W.J. Cash. Richard M. Weaver described Dixie as a land of "older religiousness" marked with a "noncreedal faith," and H.L. Mencken disparagingly pegged it "the Bible Belt."

In 2004, Fr. Paul Yerger explained Southern Christianity as "split down the middle, head and heart divided asunder. There is head religion: some tincture of Calvin, all about law and judgment, righteousness and sin, the fearful grace of the sovereign God tamed by respectability. Then there is heart religion: Pentecost, revivals, Jesus and the Holy Ghost called forth on demand to save souls and soothe the heartaches of life. And there are redneck existentialists, too, who want nothing of either."

Certainly, Dixie "held on," as educator Dr. Robert Peters put it, "while their Northern counterparts fell into heterodoxy – neo-Arianism, Unitarianism, and Universalism." But "the metaphysical bedrock of Southern culture" – traditionalist yet splintered faith ways – didn't cut it then and it sure ain't going to cut it now. If there's no shared dogma nor consistent doctrine, rites, and rituals holding together the South's Christianity, Dixie's ethnos is not only weak, it is virtually nonexistent.

In discussing the life of the aforementioned Richard M. Weaver, Professor David Middleton wrote, the political philosopher "noted, the South – which once had been 'in the curious position of having been right without realizing the grounds for its rightness' but which nonetheless by this same unarticulated instinct for the permanent things had functioned as America's 'flywheel' to check or urge on the country as a whole as it deviated from traditional values – this very South was now capitulating to a debased vision of the world presented to it in Northern books and magazines." And that was back before cell phones, Netflix, and internet porn!

Middleton continued, the South had "an attitude which Weaver believed, deprived the South of a coherent intellectual understanding of its culture... and an 'older religiousness' that shied away from theological speculation and debate, but which valued Scripture over science and which instinctively recognized and respected the natural order as God-given, mysterious, and largely unalterable by man."

As Potter said, "As have very many other Europeans over the years," the Spanish historian, Salvador de Madariaga, "once undertook a study of the War Between the States. At the end of it, he asked, referring to the South, 'Why didn't they try again?' That is, he perceived that the South's struggle was a nationalist one, and he was thinking of European peoples like the Poles and Hungarians who would revolt every 50 years until they finally achieved independence. The South did not do that."

Why? Because even though the Southern tradition was right on morals, it was drastically wrong on theology. With such a gaping chink in its armor, Dixie simply could not respond effectively to Enlightenment criticisms that became increasingly radical as time went on. It's time to try again.

This is our time to get it right by resisting the social inertia of Gnosticism. We must finally understand that we're not fighting a culture war but a spiritual one. The only choice is Christ or chaos, so we must renew our faith to reinvigorate our ethnos. To be rooted in Christ, we must reorient not East but home to Orthodoxy – the first and last bastion of Christendom.

Historian Dr. Boyd Cathey warned, "We must stand for – we must dwell within – our Citadel, our inheritance and culture, our very identity and being as a people representing 2,000 years of Western Christian heritage, or we shall disappear into the abyss of history." He's correct, but we must be precise in defining exactly what that heritage is and from whence it came.

"Never, never, never let anyone tell you that, in order to be Orthodox, you must be Eastern. The West was fully Orthodox for a thousand years, and her venerable liturgy is far older than any of her heresies." — St. John of Shanghai and San Francisco

You often hear Dixians saying, "History didn't just begin yesterday." We recognize that Americans suffer from both short-term memory and short attention spans. So, when it comes to our identity, we realize a firm handle on the past is pivotal. There's nothing more Southern than that. But there's also a distinctly Christian relationship between history and truth.

Dixie not only has (little-o) orthodox roots, but to many a Southerners' surprise, our homeland already has (big-O) Orthodox roots, too. Every Christian shares in common the spiritual ancestors of the Bible. We also share in the forebears of early Christianity, not just the Apostles, but the martyrs, Church Fathers, Saints, kings, queens, dessert dwellers, soldiers, slaves, and the fools for Christ – the entire cloud of witnesses. For the first millennia of the faith, there was but one single Church. The first Europe was Orthodox, and this was some 1,000 years before the advent of Roman Catholicism and 1,500 years prior to the Protestant Reformation.

It was a pre-denominational Christianity that was proclaiming, building, maintaining, and spreading the faith of the New Testament tradition. This wasn't a time of apostasy, as some Protestants allege, but rather a time of piety, precision, and strength. As persecution spread the Gospel, devout believers continued to evangelize across the far reaches of the Roman Empire, reaching deep into Western Europe, the British Isles, Northern Africa, and the Scandinavian lands. Western civilization wasn't born in a vacuum, randomly in Rome in 1054 or in Wittenberg in 1517. It not only has a Creator, it has a lineage. We are its progeny.

"The preservation of society is directly linked with the recovery of knowledge." — Richard M. Weaver

Common refrains in Orthodox prayers and hymns are "Unto generation and generation" and "from generation to generation," speaking to God's statutes as the inheritance for everyone, past, present, and future. And in the Gospel of Mark, "this generation" refers "to all believers at all times (i.e., the generation of the Church), and not merely those alive at the time of Christ," instructs the Orthodox Study Bible. Many Orthodox prayers end with "Both now and ever, and unto the ages of ages.

Amen." This speaks to continuity, an unbroken circle of right Christian beliefs and traditions.

Unfortunately, too many Americans are presentists when it comes to faith. As a co-founder of the Ludwell Orthodox Fellowship, which aims to *nurture the roots of Orthodoxy in Dixie's Land*, I've been called a "traitor" and "Yankee scum." I have been accused of trying to "meme Appalachia into Eastern Orthodoxy" by caustic Southerners. I have been labeled a "Lost Causer" and a "cosplayer" who is "pushing an immigrant religion" by a few haughty Orthodox. Some have called me a "Russian asset." Crass secular-humanists use even more demeaning terms.

Being told you're "pushing a foreign religion" is nothing new for an Orthodox Christian. The powerful and plentiful pagans who attacked early-Church believers and fed them to the lions were experts at this deflection. Some sincere seekers also have their Western-imposed stumbling blocks, like an acquaintance of mine who's inquiring into Orthodoxy. He recently told me, "The psychological impediment for me is more cultural than theological. It feels like 'going East' represents abandoning civilization."

This mistaken thinking would subsequently imply that those who are outside of a particular region are partaking in a foreign religion simply because we were born a great distance from where it actually began. That is silliness. As the spiritual heritage of *all* Christians, Orthodoxy offers us ties that bind beyond the geographic, political, and temporal.

If Orthodoxy is *foreign* in its pedestrian understanding, why then does the Battle Flag bear a St. Andrew's Cross? Are Southerners and their Scottish forefathers just playacting as 1st Century Middle Easterners when they pay homage to the Apostle Andrew who was crucified on an x-shaped cross?

Are Confederates of the Pee Dee Rifles considered heretics since their flag read "Under This Sign We Will Conquer" – the English translation of Emperor Constantine's phrase "In Hoc Signo Vinces" which was introduced when the Christian cross became the new standard of the Roman army in 312 A.D.?

Or is Mary Custis Lee a cultural appropriator because she sewed the stars on her husband's headquarters flag in a pattern meant to symbolize ancient Israel's Ark of the Covenant? Of course not. This flag makes perfect sense to an Orthodox Christian who understands that God revealed a pattern of worship to Moses that Christ and the Apostles practiced. We are simply the spiritual descendants of that gift.

Do I want my Southern brothers and sisters to become Orthodox? Absolutely. But make no mistake, my words aren't solely an evangelistic plea. They're also pragmatic. A right faith is *the* preeminent step in moving forward with a Southern Nationalist movement, dwarfing any other strategy or goal. "The schism in the Southern soul… will only heal when the South turns away from the Great Schism of 1054 that tore Western Europe away from the Orthodox Church and doomed her and her offspring to worldliness: wars, money-lust, falling away from God, and such like," wrote Garlington.

As a framework of classical liberalism, pluralism is the South's Achilles Heel. "American religious culture" hasn't just become flimsy and fluid. What's left of it is hostile to Christ and spiritually abusive to conservative Christians.

"It happened that a tentative experience has thrown so much light upon a bad system as to reopen discussion with better guidance than the previous."
– Robert Lewis Dabney

Honestly, a Satan-occupied Dixie would not be possible without both the Enlightenment and the Social Gospel. Post-modernity and post-Christianity are overwhelmingly "liberal Protestant," while Roman Catholicism is neoliberal due to its worldly focus on rationalism and empiricism. Both Western faith traditions are tainted by nominalism: the belief that universals are nonexistent except for in the mind.

"The denial of universals carries with it the denial of everything transcending experience," Weaver explained in *Ideas Have Consequences* in 1948. "The denial of everything transcending experience means inevitably – though ways are found to hedge on this – the denial of truth. With the denial of objective truth there is no escape from the relativism of 'man as the measure of all things'… [and] initiating a course which cuts one off from reality. Thus began the 'abomination of desolation' appearing today as a feeling of alienation from all fixed truth."

Weaver posited that the decline of Western civilization can be traced back to the ascent of nominalist thought in England during the 14th century. Although vulnerable to physical attack during the Sacking of Constantinople in 1204, Byzantium would be insulated from this scholastic scourge a century later due to its geographic position in the East. Providence, indeed. Sadly, nominalism grew in the West and has become the default position for many Christians outside of Orthodoxy.

I've heard it said that while Orthodoxy has maintained the New Testament tradition, Catholicism "added to it" and Protestantism "subtracted from it." One is top-down, making it too centralized, while the other is order-less, making it too wildly anarchic. Yet, each in its own way has become immersed in egalitarianism and democratic relativism – the same kind of perennialist thought the Yankee Empire first pushed on the South and is now exporting around the world in order to destroy more cultures and wash away the distinctions of more nations.

Writer Casey Chalk said that today's Dixie is a place "desperate for something solid and grounded, especially as we rip up and tear down monuments to our once beloved heroes... Without saints both secular and religious, our catechesis in right living is terribly impoverished." A Southern nation needs a Christian cultural permanence.

"Orthodoxy is the only Church that puts it all together: the mind and the heart, the body and the spirit, the word and the image, grace and freedom, the good God who loves mankind," Yerger proclaimed. "This is the 'evangel': the Good News for the South. Her deepest longings are met here… all that is good and true in Southern Protestantism is here. Jesus and the Holy Ghost are here: the real Jesus confessed as Lord and God and Saviour, risen from the dead." He added: "We are steeped in the Bible and love to hear its cadences. We also know that deep sense of the irony and mystery of human life, that yearning for something lost. The writers of the Bible knew this yearning well: By the waters of Babylon we sat down and wept, when we remembered Zion."

The Ludwell Orthodox Fellowship to which I belong is named after 18th Century, Colonel Philip Ludwell III. The colonial Virginian realized the facts and Orthodox faith well before the Unitarian, Transcendental, Rationalist, and Dispensational philosophies forced their way down South. A kin to some of the Southland's greatest men, such as George Washington and Robert E. Lee, Ludwell was received into Eastern Orthodox Christianity in 1738, making him the first known Orthodox convert in the Americas.

Ludwell practiced his faith in secrecy and solitude while serving in the House of Burgesses, serving in the Royal Governors Council, and living amongst his mostly Anglican or Deist contemporaries. Still, he remained faithful to the Church, leading his daughters to Orthodox conversion on Holy Wednesday 1762. The colonel (a militia title in Colonial Virginia) even translated into English a catechism, some Liturgical and confessional services, and prayers.

The rationale of the fellowship states, "The Orthodox Church teaches that there is one human family, derived from the old Adam and recapitulated in the New, and that the Orthodox Faith is for all people in all places at all times... Nonetheless, Christ, in his Great Commission, bid his disciples to 'go into all the world and make disciples of all nations (ethnoi).' From the day of Pentecost, when visitors to Jerusalem first heard the Gospel in their own languages, the Church has recognized that the one human family is composed of many distinct peoples, each of which has an absolute claim on the promises of Christ and his Church." In other words, Orthodoxy is respectful of the concept of a single human origin but is uniquely nationalistic at the same time, recognizing Godly ethnic distinctions.

Orthodox Christianity is "the best and most reliable way to preserve and support your national character." — St. Tikhon of Moscow

The Orthodox Church is worldwide by nature, but *The Basis of the Social Concept of the Russian Orthodox Church* states that "does not mean that Christians should have no right to national identity and national self-expressions. On the contrary, the Church unites in herself the universal with the national." It's the perfect balance.

Universal, yes, but decentralized and comprised of many Autocephalous National

Churches, which act under the purview of metropolitans, bishops, and other clergy, in accordance with canon law and Church traditions. This includes the laity as part of the Church governmental structure. It's both bottom up *and* hierarchical, locally enculturated *and* mystically ordered, collective *and* individual. This is something all Southern Nationalists should be able to appreciate.

"The patriotism of the Orthodox Christian should be active," the *Basis* document goes on. "It is manifested when he defends his fatherland against an enemy, works for the good of the motherland, cares for the good order of people's life through, among other things, participation in the affairs of government. The Christian is called to preserve and develop national culture and people's self-awareness."

Homeland weaves itself into the fabric of the Orthodox faith. You can love the earthly homeland that "raised, distinguished, honored, and equipped you with everything," said St. John of

Kronstadt, while simultaneously recognizing that such love does not dwarf your "special love for the heavenly homeland" which is "more precious than this one, because it is holy, righteous and incorruptible."

More than anything, the Yankee Empire fears nations reawakening to Christianity. This is why it mercilessly subjected our ancestors to invasion, conquest, occupation, and Reconstruction. This also explains why it continues to wage a religious war on the Southern spirit, especially when it sees Dixians returning to their Orthodox roots. This is how you know the Church is our protectorate: because the people who hate you and want you dead hate it so much.

Orthodoxy has stayed true to the traditions that have been handed down. Likewise, Dixie stood firm in its commitment to the Founding principles. Our Southern forebears returned to America's origins with the Confederate Constitution. The Preamble invoked "the favor and guidance of Almighty God." They understood that without virtue, a people cannot be self-governing. And you can't have virtue without the right religion – a truth which is anathema to a manufactured nation-state predicated on progressivism.

"Politics is essentially spiritual warfare carried out on the human level." — James Perloff

The most profoundly Christian of the Agrarians was Andrew Lytle who in 1980 said, "I can't believe that any society is strong which holds physical comfort as its quest. There is only one comfort, and it is the only thing that has been promised: the gates of Hell will not finally prevail."

He understood that with lethargy, a people's capacity for self-government and freedom is diminished. Hence, our Southern Nationalist movement is going to be hard work. It will require creativity, personal surrender, patience, and repentance.

"Even the best intentioned patriots, once infected, become either the Behemoth's fodder or its unwitting serfs," Dr. Marshall DeRosa notes of the "disease of centralization." Yet, what ails "us" can't be cured through secession and pure politics alone. Radical Christianity can be our medicine if we let the Orthodox Church be the hospital.

Of course, there can be temporary political successes and even triumphs that may seem long-term. Enhanced local and regional power, homeschooling, nullification, interposition, homesteading, creating alternative systems and parallel economies, decoupling from all that is hedonistic, and eventually separatism. We can and should secede in our minds *and* secede socially when and where we're able. It's that kind of resistance to conformity that is necessary to start breaking our chains to the dark principalities in high places. But it's only part of the battle.

While the Yankee Empire gasps for breath, why not fix Dixie's disparate dogmas, willy-nilly worship, and a knee-jerk nominalism that has for too long made the South defenseless and instead breathe life into right religion? There's no better time to get back to the basics than during an age of crisis. Weaver wrote, "The basis of an organic society is a fraternity which unites parts that are distinct." Orthodoxy can and should be that glue. After all, without the Church, there is no real lasting solution. To have staying power, we must build upon a rock, not shifting sand. Thus, we must be wise builders.

Southern Nationalism cannot be our version of the Tower of Babel. Will the circle be unbroken? Nope, because Orthodoxy is our second chance. By and by, Lord, by and by.

I heard it said by a priest that Orthodoxy propagates in the South like a native plant. So, let's baptize what's here, return our people back to Christ, and illumine them to the authentic Church. If we tend to and strengthen our fig tree (or in Dixie's case, perhaps it's a black walnut, black gum, persimmon, peach, or pecan tree), we will bring forth spiritual fruits and nurture our beloved homeland and ready ourselves for our heavenly home.

But before we can have a revolution in independence, we need a revolution in our conscience and a total paradigm shift. Like the great patriot and Presbyterian preacher Dabney warned, "To educate the mind without purifying the heart is but to place a sharp sword in the hands of a madman."

To create the moral integrity of a viable and enduring nation, we must have an unshakeable moral foundation and conform our lives to the moral world around us – to the natural and mystical Trinitarian law – not reconfigure the world to our desires. It's a holistic approach that regenerates us to the sacramental needs and pious particularities that our Dixie republic has for so long been lacking. *That* is our purchase on Christianity and how we attain our civilizational reality, where we not only survive, but thrive. "Nationalism" isn't the panacea, y'all. But restoring our ethnos is.

Making Secession a Reality: A Strategy, *By Padraig Martin*

"Whereas the right of peoples and nations to self-determination is a prerequisite to the full enjoyment of all fundamental human rights... The States Members of the United Nations shall uphold the principle of self-determination of all peoples and nations..." United Nations General Assembly, Seventh Session Resolution Adopted on the Reports of the Third Committee, "The right of peoples and nations to self-determination," Section A, 16 December 1952

"Give us the future... we've had enough of your past... give us back our country to live in—to grow in... to love." – Michael Collins to the British Occupiers of Ireland, The Irish War of Independence 1918 – 1922

"Invite the people to resist and be present at the scene so that with their presence the job is done." – Grand Ayatollah Ruhollah Khomeini

I am often asked, "How do we succeed? How do we win?" These questions come in a variety of ways, be they social media posts or pointed questions at various interpersonal meetings. The question is a big one to answer and I am not sure that I am big enough to answer it. The best I can do is provide a template based upon historical analogies with some practical guidance as to how to realize the goals. In this regard, I am drawing from my own education and experience to use two seemingly disparate examples for Southerners to consider as it pertains to examples of successful nationalist independence models: (1) Ireland at the turn of the 19th/20th Centuries and (2) Iran from 1978 – 1983.

The former seems natural for Southerners; the latter seems an odd fit. Yet the two examples provide extraordinary blueprints for our people. If we want to win, we should adopt strategies that make sense given our current situation. We have a right to carve out our own destiny. We should do just that.

Southern Nationalism is an ideology predicated on a foundational principle that the Southern People are unique on the North American continent – a distinct people – who have the absolute right to self-determination and the preservation of their traditions, history, and culture.

It is through this understanding of the South that Southern Nationalists believe the South has a right to be free. This is not up for debate among Southern Nationalists.

Before we can work toward any goal of independence, however, it is important to know whether Dixie even wants to be free. We know by virtue of voting records that most of the Southern people sought Dixie's independence in 1860/61. The majority in every state within the Confederacy peacefully voted for secession. The result of that conscious decision by the voters to depart from the union is well-known.

The desire to peacefully leave a voluntary union of independent countries – states – motivated the North to invade the South. They launched a terribly cruel war against the people within the Confederacy. Ultimately, they subjugated the South by means of barbarity and subsequent abusive occupation. In fact, so heinous was the assault on a free people that Yankee apologists have attached a false claim regarding black emancipation to justify their war crimes. No such motivation existed from 1861 – 1865. It was always about raw power, but I digress.

Since 1865, the South has remained a prisoner within these United States. Occasionally, the South has been gifted periods of respite, but those moments have been short-lived intervals usually at a time of war. More often than not, the Southern people have been treated as a second-class citizenry. Her people are mocked and humiliated. She is kept a prisoner designed to provide janissaries to wars that benefit Northern interests. This is not a relationship of equals. The South remains in a suspended state of rebellion whether she realizes it or not.

If we seek to successfully determine our own political and national fate, organized Southern Nationalists must adopt a strategy that empowers rebellion to break free from its suspension. This means that we must create the conditions for revolution such that the Southern people decide that the union within which they find themselves captive is no longer viewed as acceptable. This will take work, but it can be done.

In June 2021, a *Bright Line Watch* poll[31]indi cated that support for regional balkanization was at a near record high. That same poll indicated that 44% of the South supported secession, including 66% of self-identified Republicans and 50% of self-identified Independents. More surprisingly, according to the same poll, 39% of residents in the Western portions of these United States (California, Oregon, Washington, Hawaii, and Alaska) also support secession.

The matter of state secession is often derided as unrealistic. Many of our detractors will point toward the Articles of Confederation or the comments of James Madison in the 1830s. The most pointed criticism often comes from those who cite *Texas v. White*, a Supreme Court case in 1868.

---

[31] Bright Line Watch Organization, "Still miles apart: Americans and the state of U.S. democracy half a year into the Biden presidency: Bright Line Watch June 2021 surveys," (extracted 16 March 2023), http://brightlinewatch.org/still-miles-apart-americans-and-the-state-of-u-s-democracy-half-a-year-into-the-biden-presidency/

What they fail to realize are two key points. First, the Articles of Confederation, which had a union in perpetuity clause, was nullified by the ratification of the Constitution, which does not have a perpetuity clause. Second, *Texas v. White* never tackled the legality of secession when the case was brought forth regarding the status of wartime bond sales. Rather, Chief Justice Salmon Chase, who wrote the opinion of the majority in favor of the reconstruction government of Texas, effectively stated that the issue of secession was decided on the battlefield – thus, a moot point without legal merit. That stated, he also wrote, "The union between Texas and the other States was as complete, as perpetual, and as indissoluble as the union between the original States. There was no place for reconsideration, or revocation, *except through revolution, or through consent of the States.*"[32] (Emphasis my own.) In other words, Chase established that a state could leave the union by

---

[32] U.S. Supreme Court, Texas v. White Et Al, December 1868, Paragraph 101 of the majority opinion, https://www.law.cornell.edu/supremecourt/text/74/700

means of a successful revolution or through the consent of the majority of the other states within the union. It is the latter that we seek.

A peaceful divorce from an abusive federal architecture is desired by Southern Nationalists. This would first require a majority of the Southern people to desire that divorce. Then, we would need the rest of these United States to agree to our separation. Given recent polling and a deeply divided political environment, I do not believe that such an outcome is out of reach. To achieve the latter goal, we simply need to push the political envelope as far to the right within our respective states such that the other states – i.e., "blue states" – seek our extrication from the union in hopes of forming the globalist or Marxist utopia they desire. The former, however, will take a little more work, but we are closer than we think.

The following are the steps I believe we must take to realize a secession that will succeed.

Begin with defining ourselves

The challenge for Southern Nationalist entities is that we seek secession within states that have very large populations of minorities who fear a divorce from a federal government that has heretofore been their benefactors. In other words, black voters who comprise 25 – 30% of nearly every Southern state can hinder progress toward a peaceful divorce from the rest of the United States. The exceptions are Texas, Tennessee, and Florida, of which less than 17% of each state is black. (Correspondingly, these are the only three states in the South without a state income tax.) Mississippi, by contrast, is nearly 40% black. Texas and Florida have Hispanic populations that are approximately 40% and 27% respectively. Consequently, Southern Nationalists need to define themselves in such a way that they do not hide from their clearly defined, Anglo-Celtic Christian roots, but do not threaten minorities who would oppose secession, if they believed that would result in their subjugation.

For many reasons, this is why the antifa and other leftist political actors define Southern

Nationalists as "evil racists." It helps keep the threat of "neo-Confederacy" present among blocs of political allies comprised of racial minorities throughout the South. The emphasis by political opponents of Southern Nationalism avoids LGBT themes in their activism throughout most of the South, with the exceptions of Florida and Virginia. Those two states have large concentrations of cosmopolitan transplants who generally support LGBT socio-political objectives (such as the residents in or around Miami, Orlando, and Washington, DC). By contrast, leftist reactions toward pro-White or pro-Christian activism in the rest of the United States often centers around sexuality to galvanize support. Such anti-Christian sexualization does not play as well among often more culturally conservative Southern blacks.

Correspondingly, the emphasis of leftist outreach in the South is largely predicated on fearmongering over "Jim Crow 2.0." Monuments, battle flags, and other cultural reminders of the 19th and 20th centuries are used to undermine Southern

Nationalist messaging. It does not matter that Southern Nationalists have no interest in reestablishing slavery or even Jim Crow Laws. The threat is highlighted.

Southern Nationalists, even those with the most hardened racial perspectives, need to be extremely disciplined in their messaging if they want to achieve their strategic objectives. It is perfectly fine to be "pro-White" and "pro-Christian." It is important, however, to minimize communications that are "anti-others." Southern Nationalists need to define themselves as a movement that simply believes self-rule is better than rule by New York, California, and Illinois.

The outrageously anti-Christian policies of Washington, D.C., provide an excellent opportunity to Southern Nationalists. Transgenderism has been an incredible gift for our movement, and we need to exploit that fact. Pointing toward sexualized children, the mutilation of minors, and sexual confusion should be hyper-focused in drawing a distinction between the morally superior South and the other states that enjoy child disfigurement as a function of law. This is non-threatening to minorities – many of whom agree with these positions – while simultaneously avoiding racialist arguments that become messaging entrapments.

The positives of nationalism need to define us. The Irish had a similar challenge at the turn of the 20th century. Large blocs of minority Protestants were fearful of an Irish Catholic ascendancy and the potential for post-independence retribution. This fear was exploited in Northern Ireland, leading to decades of strife and violence. Meanwhile, in the South – the Republic of Ireland – Irish Nationalists made a concerted effort to invite Irish Protestants to the table. In fact, the flag itself represents an olive branch offered by the Irish Catholic majority to the Irish Protestant minority: green represents the Irish Catholics, orange represents the Irish Protestants, and white represents peace between the two.

At no time did the Irish Catholics who led the War of Independence surrender their Catholic identity or subordinate their right to freedom to placate Protestant minorities. They simply recognized that they needed to deal with a Protestant minority in a practical way. Similarly, Southern Nationalists, unlike generic White Nationalists from other areas of these United States who do not have this problem, need to find a way to at least ameliorate the concerns of minorities in a post-United States future.

That does not mean we stop seeking secession. That does not mean we disown our racial, ethnic, and religious constructs. That does not mean we argue "Rainbow Confederate" talking points. It simply means focusing on the political message of secession and elevating our people, rather than focusing on racial antagonisms and diminishing "others."

It is time for a full-throated propaganda war to strengthen the Southern identity

Before any independence movement can occur, we must build a Southern Nationalist Consensus. Southerners must be made to feel two things: uniqueness and oppression. A coordinated communications effort must be made to inculcate the Southern people with a sense of unique identity. This is fairly easy to do. Southerners already have pride in their identity. What needs to be broken from them is their attachment to an American identity that runs parallel to their Southern identity. This is where the concept of "oppression" comes to play.

As Southern Nationalists, it is not enough to simply ensure that the Southern people feel a sense of pride in who they are and what they can be. They must also know that the status quo is unacceptable. We must articulate in ways that resonate within their naturally conservative zeitgeist that the generic American affiliation is one of humiliation and suppression. At the same time that our communications strategy is focused on exemplifying the South, we must work to show every example of an American empire that is at war with our exceptional people.

While teaching Southern history to our children and introducing them to heroes, it is imperative that we also teach them that the Yankee military apparatus is tearing down monuments to those great men and stripping their names from positions of prominence. *This is not a military you should ever join...* While teaching about the virtues of Southern honor, valor, and beauty, hyper emphasize Yankee media depictions of exaggerated and grotesque Southern caricatures. *You are a beautiful Southern belle, but this movie made by Yankees depicts your people as ugly and slovenly...* The rhetorical war must be unrelenting, constant, and come from every conceivable angle. This was crucial to the success of the Irish.

Overcoming mental, psychological, and emotional hurdles to independence are difficult. The seeds of Irish independence were sown over generations of Irish Nationalists building a Nationalist consensus. An investment in Irish independence from English occupation and oppression required Irish Nationalists to break an obscure mentality of their own people. It is hard to fathom now, but at the turn of the 20th century,

Irish citizens fought dutifully for the British Crown in disproportionate numbers. While simultaneously remaining the subject of Anglo ridicule and hating the very crown for which they willingly gave their lives to defend, the Irish yielded the second largest number of recipients of the Victoria Cross (the UK's version of the Medal of Honor) after only the English themselves. Proportionately, the Irish gave more of her native sons to the British Empire than the English. That love-hate relationship with a government that loathes its most loyal fighting citizenry should be familiar to Southerners.

Beginning in the mid-19th Century, Irish Nationalists began building a network designed to sell the Irish on the notion that independence was in their personal best interest. This was very apparent during the Famine years of the late 1840s, but emigration and death were more immediate matters that had to be addressed. Still, Irish Nationalists used the Irish Famine as a rallying point at which degradation at the hands of their British oppressors was effectively exploited by a core group who made a simple, but effective argument: This would not have happened if we ruled ourselves. Think about this in our own context.

The Covid lockdowns, rampant urban criminality, transgender-inspired child mutilation, abortion… all of these are Yankee policies imposed on Southerners. It was Southern governments that have pushed back. Southerners should feel a similar sense of desire for "self-rule" that the Irish felt when they were scourged by British policies.

By the close of the 19th Century, Irish Nationalists opened Irish language schools, Irish newspapers, Irish businesses, and promoted Irish cultural icons and heroes. Irish history and legends played a crucial role in building Irish Nationalism. We need to do the same.

The combination of communicating a disgust with the ruling status quo while simultaneously elevating the Southern people must be the focus of communications from various Southern Nationalist parties. We need not join a singular organization to achieve this goal. Rather, multiple organizations should apply their talents in a coordinated push to amplify each other's messaging.

Organize Asymmetrically

While communicating and strengthening a juxtaposed vision of positive Southern identity and negative American affiliation, it is time for Southern Nationalists to get their collective act together. For too long, however, Southern Nationalists have attempted to fight the suppressing mechanisms of the federal leviathan on the government's terms. In essence, we are much like the early American revolutionaries attempting to fight the British, using well placed lines of soldiers waiting to get mowed down by superior English discipline and training. We will not win by means of physical confrontations with antifa or attempts at coercion at various monuments. They are the institution's foot soldiers and consequently own the police and courts. Any attempt at fighting them will result in our suppression.

Rather, we should have a functional council to ensure our activities do not trip upon one another. This should be kept very high level. It should be led by men and women who set aside their egos and personal allegiances to achieve a singular goal of secession. Fears of federal intrusion should be cast aside. There is nothing illegal about advocating a peaceful, political secession. This council's core objective should be ensuring discipline within our ranks, keeping group leadership focused, coordinating targeted political and communications campaigns, sharing information downstream, and providing support for one another whenever and wherever that is possible. That is where our structural organization should end. We need to adopt a Segmented Polycentric Integrated Network (SPIN) model, whereby our messaging and loose affiliations guide the majority of seemingly organic activity at a grassroots level. This is the essence of political asymmetry.

Political Asymmetry is a method of attacking and/or advancing political causes at a granular level from seemingly multiple angles, such that they are hard to both predict and defend. It exploits holes in the more organized political Left and the establishment system. It effectively weaponizes the democratic process by making it seem as though there are more voices in alignment with a given cause. In many ways, the Left has done this for years. A small group of radicals will call for the cancellation of a given political or cultural figure for holding unacceptable views. That small group is then amplified in ways that are larger than they really are, eventually effecting a result. Still, those are targeted, sustained attacks in the open. They are not asymmetric in nature. They are conventional. We need to appear larger while remaining smaller.

Since the Right enjoys larger ideological support than the political Left among the broader population, but remains far less organized, the implementation of seemingly disjointed, unaffiliated advances should be the method employed by Southern Nationalists. A smaller number of dissidents can quickly galvanize support among a conservative citizenry in such a way that leads to meaningful revolutionary reform. Grand Ayatollah Ruhollah Khomeini and his Islamic Revolution in Iran presents a beautiful case study for such a model.

Contrary to popular American mythology, the 1953 overthrow of socialist Prime Minister, Mohammad Mosaddegh, is not the origin point of current hostilities between Iran and the United States. Rather, it was the decadent 1963 White Revolution that not only caused much of the rift between modern Iranian leaders – including the deceased Khomeini – and the US. The White Revolution – inspired by American neoliberals – were a number of reforms designed to greatly liberalize Iran, largely at the expense of the conservative clergy. Betrayed by American duplicity, the 1963 White Revolution introduced similar land reform proposals as those issued by Mosaddegh. That did more to infuriate the Iranian clerical leadership which had supported the removal of Mosaddegh ten years earlier.

Beyond collectivist economic reforms, the White Revolution introduced liberalized female dress, women's suffrage, nationalized social welfare benefits, women's rights to industrial inheritance, and even gay rights. In essence, Iran became a laboratory of modernity, imposed by the US before the US made its own cultural changes. Ayatollah Khomeini saw right through it. The clergy and traditional elements were outraged.

Standing in defiance of Yankee liberalization and political interference in the mid-1960s, Khomeini was eventually arrested and then exiled by the Shah – an American puppet. In exile, Khomeini began building a dissident movement through the use of speeches recorded on easily smuggled cassette tapes and written books that were easily shared. In effect, he used communications to build a religious-nationalist identity (although Khomeini abhorred nationalism as antithetical to Islam). He built a vision of a conservative political

Shi'ite future which made suppression impossible because it resonated in the hearts and minds of those who heard or read the message. Too many young men began to look around at an unrecognizable, westernized Iran and new something had to be done. Khomeini offered them the alternative.

For Southerners trained to hate Muslims, many will recoil at the idea of learning anything from the "hated" Iran. Set aside Yankee propaganda and consider the lessons that can be learned from 1970s Revolutionary Iran. I do not believe Islam is my "friend." I am a Christian.

That stated, I believe Khomeini's lessons are important for us to learn and emulate. Through compelling messaging and asymmetric organization, the Iranian Revolution was made possible despite the overwhelming domestic intelligence apparatus of Sâzemân-e Ettelâ'ât va Amniat-e Kešvar (SAVAK). We can do the same.

Like the Iranian revolutionaries of the late-1970s, we are currently within a police state. We know that the United States government exploits various "anti-terrorism" acts to spy on its own people. We know that the United States government weaponizes disinformation to betray the American people through social media – evidence of which having recently been shared by Twitter's Elon Musk. Like all failing states, as it gets closer to full collapse, domestic intelligence operations are expanded and become more ruthless. The FBI and the DOJ have become *de facto* tools of American oligarchs, ignoring their Constitutional obligations as they target and suppress American dissidents.

Additionally, state sponsored degeneracy became hallmarks of the Shah's Iran and the current United States government. Systemic attacks on conservative virtues share similarities because their origin points are born from the same secularization goals of neoliberal policy makers. The 1963 White Revolution was an attempt to break Iran from its deeply embedded Shi'ite identity. This was led by

American and other Western actors who never fully understood how critical Shi'a Islam, especially the Jafari School of Islam, is to the Iranian people's understanding of themselves. Rather, Westerners hoped to make Iran into a Persian version of Kemal Atatürk's Turkey. The socially liberal ideals of the White Revolution were simply part of an attempted modernization program to ensure a more pro-Western (READ "vassal state") after an inevitable collapse of authoritarian rule in Iran. Why is this important? Southerners can empathize with this cultural assault.

The US is targeting its own people through socially perverted policies that undermine Christian values. From the litany of anti-Christian, pro-LGBT programs – be they flags at embassies or Congressional endorsements of sexually degeneracy – to "gender affirming" care for minors to the application of Marxist inspired Critical Race Theory, the assault on conservative norms is systemic. These policies, like the earlier attempts at secularizing Iran, are directly contrary to the moral values of the majority of the American population. They are being driven by a very small number of policy makers who have very little understanding of the broader American population – especially in the South. Just as Shi'ite identity is integral to Iranian identity, so too is Christian identity to Southern identity. Correspondingly, and inevitably, two groups will emerge, one that seeks to maintain the trajectory of immorality (the Left) and one that seeks its reversal (the Right). The United States is collapsing. The group that enjoys a stronger message among a revolutionary populace will eventually emerge victorious in a post-United States country.

In fact, that is exactly what happened in Revolutionary Iran. Two groups emerged, despite SAVAK, at a similar time in Iranian history as to that which we are currently experiencing in the US – the pre-collapse of the ruling class: Mojahedin-e-Khalq (MEK), the Marxist group responsible for the American Embassy Hostage Crisis (i.e., the socialist

Left that supported many of the White Revolution reforms) and Khomeini's Shi'ite ascendancy.

The former group, MEK, had external support for its activities. It had organization. It had all of the elements of legitimacy. Yet, it failed. Why? Because Khomeini won the hearts of the people, something which the MEK failed to do. He appealed to the conservative Iranian who was dismissed and ignored by exploitative Western policy makers in Washington, London, and elsewhere. Today, Khomeini's Iranian political structure remains, while the MEK ironically continues to exist in exile thanks to the American government they once hated.

Southern Nationalists should emulate the model of communications that Khomeini used to undermine the Shah and the West. Rather than cassette tapes, we should use podcasts that resonate within the naturally conservative hearts of the Southern people. We should use written content that speaks directly to the concerns of the Southern conservative who has been marginalized by foreign (i.e., Washingtonian) policy makers. Southern Nationalists should concentrate on socially conservative values and positions that accentuate differences between Christian Southerners and foreign Yankee ideologues.

Actions that matter

My final component of this simple strategic concept regarding how we win is meaningful action. Southern Nationalists have been entrapped by meaningless struggles with predetermined outcomes for the past decade. I know because I was one of them. Charlottesville's "Unite the Right Rally" was such a trap. Exploiting our natural anger at the removal of monuments to our heroes, our political adversaries were able to define our movement for the past six years. In many ways, this is our Celtic blood reacting with heart instead of mind. It, and many other actions we have taken as a movement, are largely described as a "Highland Charge" – concentrating our aggression at the center of a seemingly soft body. Courageous as it may be, it is a failed long-term strategy.

A better solution is to become so small and nimble they cannot define us or the movement. Rather than protesting the removal of a statue, we need to make it politically unacceptable in every small Southern town to even suggest such a thing. We may not be able to keep our statues standing in large urban locations, but it needs to be a political "death sentence" for a town councilor to even suggest the removal of a memorial in his hometown. We do this through micro action at a local level.

Rather than meet as a group and attending town council meetings as members of an organization depicted as a "hate group" by the Southern Poverty Law Center (SPLC), we need to go to such meetings as concerned, independent citizens. We need to go often and frequently. Groups of "concerned citizens" should be led with messaging from the aforementioned high council, but in a way by which no particular message can be tied to any particular group. Recruitment should be in the form of an invitation after local political engagement to a bar or a coffee shop to discuss the events of the meeting. Sending out local organizers with no known external affiliation to rally around the most hard-right propositions in a given county or town should be the goal. We did this in Northern Virginia and in Central Florida with great success. The model should be replicated throughout the South.

Did you know your children are being taught Marxist-inspired Critical Race Theories that target them for being White? We must stop this immediately. Let's meet at the school board and make them answer.

Did you know the elected sheriff's new proposal would effectively end the enforcement of minor thefts in an effort to lower minority arrests? This will destroy our sense of safety and property values. Let's meet at the town council and make her answer.

Did you know your children are provided transgender support by school counselors without your consent? They cannot get away with this. Let's meet at the school board and make them answer.

This should be the focus of recruitment. Emphasizing local politics and ensuring grassroots support resonates in such a way that federal monitoring of each and every council becomes impossible. Exploiting a politician's innate desire to retain power through reelection at the local level is a powerful tool for the dissident. We may not be able to change the political outcomes of "national" elections, but we can change the future of local elections.

In addition to this, we need to create functional parallel societies. Dissidents should be engaged in the creation of farmers' markets, product exchanges, alternative arbitration courts, after school assistance, and home school collectives. Cultivating volunteers among Southern Nationalists should not be difficult. After all, everyone engaged in this movement is effectively a volunteer. We do not get paid to put ourselves on the line. Our activism comes with doxing, harassment, and often impoverishment. Let us put ourselves on the line for something that can directly help our people separate from the modern United States.

The Irish and the Iranians both created parallel infrastructures that ultimately filled the gaps within society after the ruling classes were expelled. In the Iranian case, much of the shadow governance was established by a network of financiers and the clergy, despite overwhelming surveillance by SAVAK. In the Irish case, the Irish Republican Brotherhood established a series of alternative mechanisms of government – from courts to economic resources – before the British departed "the Castle" in Dublin. Southerners need to do the same for two reasons. First, it inspires confidence that the alternative – a Free and Independent Dixie – will remain functioning after the ruling class is dismantled. Second, it empowers our people.

Finally, there needs to be meaningful "national" engagement by legal "calls to action." Southern Nationalists should periodically encourage – without warning – their followers to take actions that are legal but meaningful. This is where the previously mentioned SPIN strategy gains its greatest effect.

Rather than holding concentrated rallies, the rally should be a call to action for a given political or social messaging campaign. Communications need to be targeted, disciplined and stay within the confines of the law. The following is such an example.

There should be no greater cause for Southern Nationalists than fundamentally devastating American military recruitment. From a strategic perspective, this must be a priority. Too many young Southern men continue to join a United States military that hates them, largely because they are encouraged by their fathers and grandfathers who are nostalgic for a military that existed in the 1980s, not the 2020s. Communications, therefore, need to focus on the fathers and grandfathers, not their sons who are impressionable.

Southern Nationalists should pick periods of peak military recruitment (early Fall and early Spring) to target Home Depot, Lowes, or church parking lots with fliers that stay focused on undermining military recruitment. Historical reenactment sites are rife with our targeted demographic. Such a call to action should be simple. A large-scale account on Gab can produce an easily printed flyer that states something to the effect: *"The US military uses Critical Race Theory in its training of military officers. Those officers will not only determine how your sons or daughters will be treated in the ranks, but whether they are promoted and/or how they will be deployed. Encourage your children to consider options other than enlistment."* A quote of General Mark Miley can be used to add weight to the message. Target parking lots with conservative leaning consumers and/or attendees.

There is nothing illegal in the message. There is nothing racist. The breadth of potential targets is too large for the antifa or anyone else to calculate and/or undermine. The sheer number of accounts that may be inspired to act are too numerous for the American domestic surveillance apparatus to monitor. Even if they tracked everyone who downloaded the image, they would not know the individual's preferred target for dissemination. *Is it Lowes or Home Depot or St. Michael's Church...?* Furthermore, the military provides ample evidence of its hatred for its once most loyal class of citizen. They literally write the propaganda for us. We just need to share that which they say or do.

Other messaging can be similarly weaponized throughout the South. Most people are not nearly as engaged politically or socially to notice policy shifts. Most of the unpopular policy shifts are not covered in the news and they are suppressed by mainstream social media sites. Consequently, getting this message out to ordinary Southerners is critical to the success of both destroying the United States' ability to continue harming our people and building a secession consensus.

The Irish employed "flying columns" comprised of small, local units that exploited the sluggish British military's cumbersome numbers and discipline. We need a similar method of attack.

I am not advocating violence. I do not want the reader to assault a military convoy on I-95. Rather, I am advocating a seemingly disjointed, mass communications action comprised of individuals who are too small and too quick to hit, sharing information that undermines the United States with its own words and deeds.

In sum, when I am asked. "How do we win," my answer is to change our strategy. We need to define ourselves, engage in an all-out propaganda campaign, and change our methods of actionable engagement. We have allowed our enemies to define us. That needs to stop.

We need to organize in a manner that is more natural for our people. We need to engage them in ways that avoid American domestic surveillance. We need to elevate them and dismantle misplaced American patriotism.

These are realistic solutions that can be employed. It will take work. But if you have the heart to be an effective Southern Nationalist, you will join me and start now.

About the Author: Padraig Martin (pseudonym) is a devout Christian who holds dual American and Irish citizenship. He is the son of an Irish mother and an American father. His American grandmother has deep roots in Virginia. His Irish grandmother played a significant role in his upbring in Ocala, Florida. Mr. Martin holds two masters' degrees from elite universities – one in Islamic Studies and the other an MBA. Padraig owns four companies with his wife on two continents. He is a dedicated Southern Nationalist and a tireless proponent of Florida secession, where he currently resides with his wife, and some of his seven children (many are grown). Padraig Martin's is prolific contributor to the online blog, Identity Dixie, the host of Dixie on the Rocks podcast, and the author of <u>A Walk in the Park: My Charlottesville Story</u>, which can be purchased through Amazon.com.